John Burns has spent over forty years exploring Britain's mountains. He has walked and climbed in the American and Canadian Rockies, Kenya, the Alps and the Pyrenees. John was a member of the Cairngorm Mountain Rescue Team and is an award-winning mountain writer. His first book, *The Last Hillwalker*, has become a bestseller and was shortlisted for TGO Book of the Year. His popular blog receives many thousands of visits and John continues to develop his career as a writer and outdoor storyteller whilst exploring the wild places he loves.

BOTHY TALES

Footsteps In The Scottish Hills

JOHN D BURNS

JOHNDBURNS.COM

Bothy Tales

Published in 2018

www.johndburns.com

Edited by Pinnacle Editorial

www.alexroddie.com/pinnacle-editorial

Cover design & interior formatting by

Mark Thomas / coverness.com

First Paperback Edition

British Library CIP

A CIP catalogue record for this title is available from the British Library

ISBN: 978-0-9955958-2-8

Contents

For my daughters, Cat and Mairi, who brought joy into my life.

With love.

*"What we get from this adventure is just sheer joy.
And joy is, after all, the end of life."*
–George Mallory

"Why go all the way up there? You'll only have to come back."
–John Elliott

Ghost Riders

If you wanna save your soul from hell a-riding on our range
Then cowboy change your ways today or with us you will ride
Trying to catch the devil's herd across these endless skies.
–Johnny Cash

It's been raining for four days now. Martin and I are saturated. Water has seeped through every layer of our clothing. The arms have fallen off my Pac-A-Mac and my overtrousers are split. I have no defence against the deluge and no alternative but to surrender to the aquatic invasion of my body. Here, on Black Hill on the Pennine Way, Martin and I are nearing exhaustion – the rain batters us mercilessly, the weight of our packs drags us down and the sheer monotony of walking hour after hour every day tests our mental resources to the limit. But it's not the rain that is our biggest enemy, threatening to bring us to a grinding halt, but a far more formidable foe: the peat.

We are trudging knee deep through a soup of saturated black ooze. Every step is torture and forward movement often becomes impossible. Sometimes it holds our boots so fast momentum carries us forward and pitches us face down into the black treacle. Weighed down by our rucksacks, it is impossible to get up – we have to wriggle out of the straps before we can rise to our feet, dripping gunge, like melancholy versions of the

Creature from the Black Lagoon.

From somewhere out in the mist we hear a cry: "Help!"

We find two walkers. One is being devoured by the peat monster; he is already up to his thighs and is sinking slowly. In broken English his friend tells us he is Dutch and all efforts to move him have failed. It seems odd to me to come all this way to the spine of England to drown in peat – surely he could have done that at home.

I grab my European cousin under the armpits and pull. Nothing happens. He is stuck firm; the peat has him in its grip. The ground around him is so liquefied no one else can get close to him and I am sinking too. Martin finds a semi-rotten plank, half embedded in the peat; I stand on it and pull again. Now I heave as hard as I can.

"Argh, my back!" the Dutchman yells in pain. I keep pulling. It's either me or the monster.

There is a tortured, gurgling sound from the peat and the Dutchman begins to move.

It's forty years since Martin and I battled the nightmare of peat to complete the Pennine Way.

On this winter's evening, we sit in front of the bothy stove, its heart glowing yellow with burning wood. The whisky and the warmth are taking hold and both of us begin to doze quietly. Outside, a ferocious wind, roaring like a beast untamed, hurls rain at the windows and tears at the roof with its claws.

This is Glen Pean bothy, at the head of Glen Dessary, not far from Fort William, in the Scottish Highlands. Despite the remoteness of this small, stone-built shelter, and the power of the storm raging across the mountains around us, Martin and I sit before the fire in the flickering candlelight enjoying a warm glow of contentment, certain in the knowledge that there is nothing too seriously wrong with the world.

Seventeen miles away, Loch Arkaig – the enormous strip of water that snakes its way down the glen, its lochside road our only exit – is swallowing thousands of tonnes of rain. The rivers have become torrents and spouts of white water plummet down the mountainsides and tumble into the loch all along its length. Swollen by the floods, the loch is rising, bursting its banks. Soon it will drown the little single-track road that runs beside it. By morning we will be marooned. That human beings are blind to the disasters about to befall them is a blessing – if we all knew our fate life would be a grim waiting game.

Martin and I have known each other since primary school, which means I've been seeing his aquiline features on and off for more than fifty years. In the early 70s we both walked the Pennine Way. Somehow, barely equipped, vastly inexperienced and way out of our depth, we completed the 270-mile walk. This evening, whilst our friend Joe (a newcomer we have only known for a little shy of fifty years) snores on the sleeping bench of the bothy, Martin and I relive the walk. We laugh at how poorly equipped we were; we had rudimentary rucksacks, no waterproofs to speak of and a tent made of bed sheets. Martin didn't even have any boots. He completed the walk in street shoes. We look back fondly on one of our first independent ventures into the hills with the nostalgia of old men remembering their youth.

I can't remember which of us said it, but the words, once

spoken, hung in the air and brought me back to reality with a start.

"Well, we could do it again," one of us suggested and, as the storm railed outside the bothy, we both fell silent.

My first book, *The Last Hillwalker*, ended with me and Martin sitting in that Highland bothy and deciding – for reasons neither of us is too clear about – to attempt the Pennine Way again. I have been amazed by readers' reactions to my first book. It has become a bestseller, and more importantly struck a chord with outdoor folk. In the book I tried to tell the story of the average hillwalker, of their love of the hills, of their lives and adventures, and it seems that, to some extent at least, I achieved this.

Rather than being satiated by writing *The Last Hillwalker*, my fascination with the landscape of the Highlands and the folk who wander these hills has deepened. When I am not chained to my PC, writing, I am exploring this wonderful land at every opportunity. When I finished my first book I realised I had more tales I wanted to tell. Some of these stories are factual accounts; others come more from the flights of a fanciful imagination. I'll leave you to decide which is which.

A lot of people asked what happened to me and Martin on the Pennine Way, forty years after our first completion, so here's the story of our second attempt.

* * *

I've been walking for a long time, so long that it's difficult to remember a time when I wasn't walking. My past life has faded into oblivion. I have become a simple organism. All I do is walk.

I no longer think – thought has become an inconvenience. I just move my legs and strike the ground with my trekking poles in a perpetual rhythm that drives me ever onwards.

Martin and I have been walking for almost twelve hours. Twenty miles lie behind us since we set off just after 8.00 a.m. from the paradise of our campsite in Crowden. Johnny Cash's song *Ghost riders in the Sky* is playing on a continuous loop through my mind. In the song he tells of ghostly cowboys, condemned to ride across endless skies in pursuit of a herd they will never catch. It feels like me and Martin walking across endless moorland in search of a trail end we will never reach.

It's May, but as we walk mile after mile across this high, empty moorland a ceaseless, cold easterly wind blows into our faces, gently but relentlessly pushing us back. It's been blowing this way for weeks and has desiccated the rolling peat landscape. Now it drains us of energy. The effort it takes to push against it is the equivalent of a couple of miles each day.

An hour ago we passed the White House pub on this, our second day on the Pennine Way.

Martin turned to me as we set off on this section that leads, past a series of reservoirs, to the village of Mankinholes. "This section is five miles long, but don't worry, it's flat. The easiest on the whole Way."

Martin is an authority on the route by now. Over the years he has repeated many of the sections we walked in our youth. He knows every twist and turn, but this section does not feel easy now. My legs remember the previous day's battle – setting out from Edale, over Kinder Scout and the dreaded Bleaklow moor. Forty years ago Martin and I crossed that moor in mist and pouring rain, floundering through a black soup of peat bog. If you want to know what Bleaklow is like the clue is in its name.

There was something unnerving about standing on the station platform in Edale where we had begun this walk half a lifetime ago. Then I felt differently. I was excited, elated, about what was to come. I was filled with the boundless energy and optimism of youth. I didn't know what I was about to face although, at 19, I was sure we could defeat whatever was ahead of us. Standing there all those years later, I knew what was ahead and the prospect filled me with dread. I know now what I did not know then: we were about to meet a monster.

The Pennine Way begins in Edale and is the big daddy of British long-distance walking routes. Back in 1974, when I walked the route with Martin, it had only been open a handful of years and stood alone as the longest, toughest walk in the UK. Now there is a plethora of coastal paths, Trails and Ways. Some are wild and remote like the Cape Wrath Trail; others longer, but broken into many short sections such as the Cornish Coast Path. None, however, can claim the status of the Pennine Way. Covering around 270 miles and running up the spine of Britain, it took an act of Parliament to create as it forced its way north, often against the opposition of land owners.

Martin and I head across the dams where the open reservoirs offer no shelter from the wind. I come to a halt. Across our path is a wire fence and a little sign saying 'diversion'. Clearly some work is being carried out on the dam, and the contractors, steeped in health and safety, want us to take the long way around the lake. Normal walkers would have happily plodded off around the rough track and taken the extra half mile in their stride. I, however, am too tired to consider an extra hundred yards.

Diggers sit silently on the other side of the fence, their drivers long since gone off for their tea, no doubt sitting in various hostelries across the county. I am unable to see anything capable of dealing sudden death and begin to climb the fence. But halfway up, I realise that I am not 19 any more as middle-aged legs, tired from walking, struggle to propel me over the barrier. It's now that I remember I am over sixty and overweight. I had planned to diet before the walk – to at least lose a little of my paunch – but I put it off and, a few weeks before, decided it was too late to do anything and kept eating the pies. Now it's time to pay.

Martin watches in silence as I teeter precariously on the high wire. He has developed a strategy over the years: he lets me go first, and if I cross the river/bog/mountain ridge without getting killed, he follows. On the odd occasion when I have slipped off stepping stones and fallen waist deep in the water he quietly heads off to find a safer route. Since I don't die on this particular occasion we both climb the fence and head off across the dam.

At last, our second day, one of the longest on the route, slowly comes to an end as we descend with aching legs towards the little village of Mankinholes. I find Joe sitting comfortably in the bar, waiting for us geriatric walkers to stagger off the moor. After so many hours of walking, exposed to the wind and plodding through bog, it feels odd to suddenly experience the shelter of walls and be surrounded by people who have not been walking for so long they have become automatons. Martin reaches for the menu and I head for the bar to buy a much-needed round of drinks. When I return, Martin is standing panic stricken on his chair whilst the pub's Jack Russell hovers for dropped chips beneath our table.

Martin has an irrational fear of dogs (and all other animals for that matter). He is fervently of the belief that animals are about to come snarling at him and inflict the most fearful injuries. The size of the creature is immaterial; he is certain that anything bigger than a hamster is capable of grievous bodily harm. Thus the innocent Jack Russell, in search of an illicit snack, sends him into a panic. Joe and I have learned to accept this and realise that no amount of rational explanation will reassure him. The overweight pub manager regards Martin's antics with rising alarm until we explain his phobia. Then he merely shakes his head and looks on, bemused.

Eventually, Martin having survived the attack of the monstrous chip-eating Jack Russell, we head off for a campsite. On our first trek up Britain's spine Martin and I carried a rudimentary tent, as we had no money to buy anything better. Now, in the luxury of middle-aged wealth, Joe possesses a small camper van and – in an act of incredible generosity – is following along our route, bringing our luggage and the facilities of his little home from home along with him. The van is too small for us all to sleep in so Joe has erected tents for me and Martin. I sleep on my top-of-the-range air mattress, cosy in my down bag and *immensely* grateful that I am not shivering in the inadequate equipment of my teenage years.

The Victorians were very fond of big pointy things. So fond that they have littered the English countryside with them. Not content with the height of the hills around them, the Victorians made many of them higher by sticking a pointy thing on top. Often, they made them memorials to some war but that's not the real reason they are there. The Victorians built them just because they could. Often it was the landed gentry who put them there. Mainly so that, after dinner during brandy and cigars, they could gesture across the landscape and explain that they were responsible for that marvellous pointy thing on the horizon.

Next morning, my legs are startled. They have just walked two consecutive long days, and fancy a lie-in while I read the papers. Unfortunately, that's not what they get. They are woken, rather rudely, and forced into boots again. Soon they are climbing the little path that leads out of the village of Mankinholes and up to Stoodley Pike where Martin and I staggered from the Pennine Way late last night. The path up from the valley is unlike anything I've seen before. It is paved and the paving stones gently curve into each other, so they have a kind of natural fit. It's almost pleasant to walk on and doesn't jar with the landscape as so many paved paths do.

As Martin and I crest the ridge the east wind meets us head on. It's been waiting for us all night and now tries, with all its vigour, to push us back to Edale. Soon we are sheltering in one of the little alcoves in the memorial at the top of Stoodley Pike. The memorial is one of the pointy things I mentioned before. It is possible to climb the steps inside it and gain an even higher elevation but neither Martin nor I feel like adding unnecessary ascent – we already have a great deal of climbing ahead of us.

The memorial was built in 1814 by public subscription. About thirty years later, wind, rain and a fair clout of lightning demolished it. The Victorians – nothing if not determined – built it back up again, only this time they had the bright idea of putting a lightning conductor in it and so here it stands today.

"We are heading over there," Martin tells me, pointing into the distance with his walking pole.

I can just make out a thin spidery line that is the path we are following. I note with growing sadness how far away it looks as the route vanishes over the horizon, doubtless seeking further hills for us to climb. From the memorial we head down towards the next valley. The Pennine Way is a long rollercoaster of a walk. You head up a hill, over its top and then down the other side. You do this repeatedly until either you die or get to the end of the walk. That sums up hillwalking in general I suppose but is especially pertinent to the Pennine Way.

As we cross the bridge over the Rochdale Canal I begin to realise that my heels don't feel right. I take off my boots and, much to my consternation, see that blisters are beginning to form. It's thirty years since I last had a blister, so long ago that I have dismissed them as a possibility. Blisters are things other people get. I don't carry anything to prevent them because they never happen. Martin (always prepared for everything) rummages in one of his countless plastic bags and produces plasters.

Across the canal the path climbs steeply up a narrow country lane surrounded by beautiful little stone cottages that look as if they grew naturally from the hillside rather than being built by the hand of man. They are full of odd angles, little ledges and twisted windows, and look as though they have stood for hundreds of years – which, of course, they probably have.

Wonderful flowers grow out of the cracks between the stones and come tumbling down from the walls, filling the warm air with their scent. It would be a kind of idyll, if we weren't climbing a near-vertical path. The Pennine Way would be fantastic if it weren't for all the bloody walking.

Half an hour later we emerge from the Calder Valley and reach the brow of the hill. I'm trying to ignore the pain that is increasingly evident in my legs,. For once I am glad of the east wind as it brings relief from the heat of the valley. Forty years have dulled my memory and I have no knowledge of ever being in this place before.

"There's a shop here," Martin calls to me.

I look around. We are standing in a field in the middle of nowhere. "There can't be. There's nothing here.'

"It's called Aladdin's Cave," he insists.

His mind has finally snapped. Now he thinks we are taking part in some Arabian Nights epic. Then, a couple of hundred yards along the country lane, a shop appears. It's one of those, 'we stock everything you've ever heard of' country shops, run by middle-aged women who bustle around the place like bees tending a hive. I should have learned by now that, where sources of refreshment are concerned, Martin is never wrong.

I walk in to this little oasis and want everything all at once: tea, sausage rolls, soup. I am overwhelmed by the splendour within. Moments later I am sitting outside in the sun with an ice cream. I am very fond of ice cream but, being a middle-aged man with a tendency to rotundness, it is a delight I rarely indulge in. Now, I decide, having walked for days, a retired gentleman should be entitled to sit on a bench in the sun and eat a bloody ice cream. Martin indulges in one of the meat and potato pies he remembers from past visits. Just for a moment we'll forget about blood pressure, cholesterol and diabetes.

To be honest I never go near doctors – once they get their stethoscopes on to you they never let go. I'll die of something, nothing is more certain, but I'd like it to come as a surprise rather than a twenty-year black cloud. When my grandfather was in his 97th year his district nurse – or at least the latest one, he'd outlived several of them – was still trying to persuade him to stop smoking. How old did she want him to be? If he's still smoking at 97 he's won, it's game over. For a few blissful minutes I am able to sit and enjoy the delicious cold sweetness of my ice cream while the pain in my blistered heels subside.

Soon we are walking again, crossing sweeping open moorland that runs to the horizon. Here the way is flagged. Now the wind finds us again and the vast area of tall grass we are walking through comes alive like a sea. Here we are overtaken by a Lycra-clad wraith of an individual, moving with such urgency I can only assume he is part of some long-distance race.

"Hello," I say, "not a bad day."

The man pauses and glares at me intently. "You have stopped," a disembodied voice says. The man rummages about in his ears and unplugs his earbuds.

"Average speed five point two kilometres per hour," the digital god speaks again. His physique is emaciated, and he carries a small rucksack crammed with his few possessions. All I can see of his face is a neatly trimmed beard protruding beneath his dark glasses.

"You have stop—" the voice begins again. This time he

fiddles with his phone and the voice ceases.

"I'm being sponsored you see," he announces in a brown sauce Brummy accent.

"Oh right."

"I continuously post my position on Facebook, so I can't stop." He fiddles with his phone again and looks at me with a haunted expression.

I feign interest, trying to reassure him. "What are you being sponsored for?"

He grins at me and then his face clouds. "Er… Well it's… It'll come back to me."

The digital voice kicks in. "You have stopped." This time it sounds accusatory.

He waves the phone at me. "Mustn't stop. It's marvellous this, tells me when I deviate more than five feet from the path. It tells me everything I need to know. Everything!"

He is already walking now. I hear the demonic voice from his phone tell him he lost time when he stopped and how fast he needs to go to catch up. He breaks into a run; soon he and the digital voice that controls him are lost in the distance.

* * *

I kneel on the step of Joe's camper van, as if in prayer, whilst he peers at my bleeding heels. We have arrived at the campsite in Cowling, and Joe is tending to the wounded.

"Well, I've seen worse." He sucks his teeth like a mechanic about to deliver a hefty estimate. "But not much worse."

Joe is an expert on blisters. For many years he was an outdoor pursuits organiser for the Duke of Edinburgh's Award.

This organisation was set up to ensure that young people get a thorough grounding in suffering. It's based on the theory that pain and discomfort are good for young people. The idea is that you find a group of teenagers, happily drinking cider and smoking cigarettes behind the bike sheds – or perhaps more accurately these days glued to social media – and take them out in the mountains where they can become cold, exhausted, and wet. After this treatment they never moan about being bored again in case an adult finds them and takes them out into the great outdoors once more. It's a laudable plan.

Most of the victims of this scheme had never been fortunate enough to tramp through miles of bog wearing ill-fitting boots until they were captured, and so suffered awesome blisters that did them the world of good. Joe, as a result, has become an expert at patching up the heels of whimpering teenagers, and knows exactly what to do with my feet.

That evening we notice our sponsored friend from earlier in the day. He's sitting in his tent stirring something in a pot when Martin attempts to talk to him. The bearded man unplugs his ears from his phone and begins to explain to Martin the technical details of how his wonder device works. This is a waste of time as Martin has never used a mobile phone in his life and will only speak on a telephone that is connected to something by wires. Undaunted, our fellow walker sets off into a long explanation about the advantages of GPS.

"I see," Martin says, who doesn't see at all, and tries to switch the conversation to something he does understand: food. "What's that you are eating?"

The man replies, and Martin spends several moments

staring into the pot with a mixture of puzzlement and wonder. After a few moments he excuses himself, and sits down beside me, deep in thought.

At length Martin turns to me. "I don't suppose you know what couscous is, do you?"

"I'm afraid I don't."

"Well," he says with a profound sigh. "Apparently people eat it."

* * *

The following day we drive to the nearest chemist and obtain medical supplies – some elasticated adhesive bandage and a dressing for burns called Melolin – and then spend a glorious day dozing and drinking tea. We set out the next morning swathed in Doctor Rigby's bandages. The next stage of our walk takes us through rolling meadows and past the tiny mill village of Lothersdale. The mill chimney stands tall above the village and a little plaque boasts that the mill has the largest indoor mill wheel in the UK. I'm aware that this fact alone may not send you into rapture but you never know when it might come in useful. You might find yourself on TV one day when that very question is asked by some ridiculously tanned celebrity and is the final barrier between you and untold wealth, or at least a nice glass trophy you can put on the mantelpiece. Then you can remember this little book and your life will be filled with joy.

At last we arrive in the village of Malham and here make the foolish error of calling in at the pub on the way back to the campsite.

"I never want to move again," I announce, sitting by the pub fire, a couple of pints of fine ale inside me, my legs exhausted. "I'll be fine, I'll just stay here in this seat for the rest of my life."

I am beginning to learn a sad fact about getting older. Martin and I can do the mileages, we can walk 24 miles in a day with few problems, but what we can't do is keep walking those distances day after day. That, I decide, must be why the army doesn't like to recruit sixty-year-old men. The teenage youths are certainly more malleable than the sixty-year-olds and they also recover a lot faster. There is no doubt that we probably have covered some sections of the walk much faster than we did forty years ago. On our first attempt it took us two days to get from Edale to Crowden; it only took us one this time. On our first walk we were so inefficient at dismantling tents and getting our gear packed we often didn't set off until eleven, frequently only making the pub at last orders.

They say 'age is only a number' – really? Try telling my legs that. Martin's left shoulder is growing increasingly painful from the constant jarring of walking poles. Each successive day is more of a struggle than the last. We are slowly grinding to a halt. At nineteen we got stronger; now, forty years on, we are slowly falling apart. Neuralgia is gradually overcoming nostalgia.

* * *

Ten days in to the walk I can move only with the aid of barrels of anti-inflammatory gel, sticking plasters and real ale anaesthetic. Martin and I descend from hours of walking to the small town of Middleton-in-Teesdale. For once the campsite we are looking for is exactly where it should be, at the end of the path as we come off the hill. I walk, stiff legged, into the campsite office and a plump, middle-aged woman looks up from her desk and can see the old timer is in trouble.

"Oh, what a shame you weren't here last week," she says, pity radiating from behind her horn-rimmed specs. "You've missed him."

I just want a shower and a place to fall over and groan for a while; I'm not expecting to meet anyone. I look at her, puzzled.

"Elvis!" she explains. "You missed Elvis."

Oh God, now I'm hallucinating.

* * *

I remember this campsite from our first trip all those years ago. Then we had come down from the hills, late as usual, and the fiftyish Geordie who ran the place took pity on us. He came out from behind the counter of the campsite bar, which was thronged with older couples and families. Come to think of it most people were older than us in those days.

"Are you boys just down from the mountains?" He drew us to him into a conspiratorial huddle. "Let me get rid of this lot', gesturing towards the caravan dwellers for whom he obviously had little affection. 'You come back and we'll have a few pints."

It was our first experience of the joys of illicit late-night drinking. Back in the 70s the little bar had seemed smart, almost plush with its velvet seats and walls festooned with horse brasses. We luxuriated in the knowledge that we were part of a select band of mountain men whom the owner considered fit to share an after-hours pint with.

Now I realise the bar is the converted station house of the Middleton-in-Teesdale to Barnard Castle line, which was closed in 1965. That evening, as we sit refuelling with beer, the campsite bar's luxurious feel has faded, and the furniture and decorations appear old and worn.

The campsite manageress (who was so disappointed at my failure to meet Elvis) comes bustling over. "Don't worry love, you missed Elvis, but there's bingo tonight." Everyone is warm and friendly and it's obvious that we have stumbled into a small community of folk for whom this little campsite is their weekend home.

"We've been coming here for thirty years," one woman boasts. It occurs to me to tell her that we've been coming here for over forty years, but I don't want to dent her pride, and smile back my admiration. These folk are not walkers but they come here with their children – and, to Martin's alarm, their dogs – to find some sanctuary from industrial towns like Durham and Sunderland. They are not so different from me and my bothy wanderings.

I decide it is time to accept reality. "We're not going to make it, are we?"

Martin doesn't answer for a while and sits sipping his cider. In the end he says, "No, we won't do it now."

We both know that, as we progress north, we will encounter longer and wilder stretches of the Pennine Way. The final stage, the biggest of them all, is 29 miles long, something neither of us feels inclined to tackle. And we are running out of time.

"I think we should bail out at Dufton, so we'll finish at High Cup Nick – that would be a really spectacular way to finish."

We have a plan. The end is only two days away.

* * *

Coming from the south, the spectacle of High Cup Nick comes as a surprise. One moment we are plodding through open moorland, battling the incessant easterly wind that has tried to drive us back for the last two weeks. It isn't gale force but it has been strong enough for us to have to fight against it every step of the way from Edale, strong enough to sap our energy and dry our skin to red raw parchment. The backs of my hands are burnt red, more by the wind than sun, and the outline of the straps on my walking poles shows where the skin is white.

The next moment we are standing by the edge of a cliff gazing out across a vast scoop in the landscape. The valley before us is edged with steep cliffs and appears perfectly symmetrical. At our feet the stream we have been following tumbles over the lip of the basin and falls into the valley below. It feels as if we are on the edge of a great volcano that has somehow been cut in half so that only the side of the crater we are standing on remains.

The geology of High Cup Nick was, of course, formed not by a long-dead volcano but by the actions of glaciation. What the ice has left behind is a classic U-shaped valley, one of the most spectacular in Britain. This is a primeval place. The view from this cliff edge is etched in my memory and I can recall it exactly as I saw it when Martin and I were here decades ago. Little has changed here in all that time, but Martin and I have been altered by time and so has our perception of the Way. Back in the 70s it seemed a wild and untamed place – now it feels like a long moorland walk. You still walk in splendid isolation for much of the route, seeing few folk outside of the villages and the tourist traps of Edale and Malham, yet that apparent isolation is an illusion: the Way weaves across moorlands with the industrial towns of northern England only just out of sight.

Since we first walked the Way I have climbed in Canada and the Alps and become familiar with the wastes of Sutherland and the wilds of the Cairngorms, so it is inevitable that the Way makes less of an impression on me than it did in my youth. Despite that, the Pennine Way is still a great iconic walk; and I am satisfied that, though we have not been able to turn back time, we have once more given ourselves lasting memories.

Joe is waiting for us in the village of Dufton where his camper van is parked. Joe has even negotiated special permission for Martin to pitch his tent in an area normally reserved for camper vans. This is so that Martin won't have to be close to a tent housing a particularly large and ferocious-looking dog. No such permission has been obtained for me; apparently it's okay if I am devoured during the night. I meet Joe in the street outside the village pub and we debate whether to head in for a beer or wait for Martin, who is a few minutes behind me. When Martin arrives he is tired as he swings his walking poles in front of him but he also appears disappointed that we didn't reach Kirk Yetholm.

I shake his hand. "Congratulations, well done."

At first he looks confused, but then he smiles – what we have just done is, in its way, a great achievement. We didn't get to the end of the Pennine Way, but we returned to walk together again after over forty years. Not many people have done that. It's half a lifetime since two long-haired youths with flared trousers and virtually no gear staggered up this route, and now we have come back. We have better gear now but we don't have nineteen-year-old legs any more.

"One hundred and sixty-two miles." Martin announces later in the pub.

"That's a long way." Even if we didn't win the race, that distance is an achievement for sixty-year-old men. Maybe we didn't make the summit, but we had a damn good try and that is enough for me. I didn't win the bingo at the campsite in Middleton-in-Teesdale, but I walked 162 miles of the Pennine Way. You can't win them all.

Later, when beer has been consumed, one of us (I can't remember which) suggests we come back and finish the walk next year. It's hard to be certain, but that may even have become a plan.

Cause they've got to ride forever on that range up in the sky,
As they ride on, hear their cry.
Yippee-yi-ay, yippee-yi-o,

Ghost riders in the sky

Faindouran

It is the emptiness of this place that impresses me. The broad glen sweeps away into the distance, and my eyes are drawn to the river, a long shimmering line, one of the few signs of movement in this cold, grey landscape. The clouds, racing across the vast Cairngorm skies, are the only other animated things. I am walking slowly but purposefully; a solitary, minute figure in this colossal place.

In most Highland glens you are enclosed by steep hills, but the wide Cairngorm valleys open up to huge skies. I have been walking for a long time, so long that the process has become mechanical, a trudge that must be endured. With each step, the east wind, rushing down the valley towards me, tries to force me back with cold, persistent pressure. My feet hurt, my legs ache, I dream of sitting down. The daylight is fading now and the hills recede to silhouettes. Many hours before, I passed Lochan Uaine (the Green Lochan) and Ryvoan bothy, and walked on, over the shoulder of Bynack More. My path then took me on through that great junction of lonely glens at the Fords of Avon. Now, I am only a few miles from my goal, the remote Faindouran bothy, but these last miles are proving hard to win.

Faindouran is different from many Highland bothies in that it is visible from a distance of several miles. Most bothies play hide and seek with you; they stay hidden until you despair and decide you must be completely lost, that the bothy is nowhere close. Then, and only then, do they pop out from behind a bush to startle you like a mischievous child. Faindouran, however, has a different strategy. On the path down Glen Avon (pronounced *aan*) it waves to you, calling you to it from far away but like some Highland mirage, no matter how far you walk, it never gets any closer.

This is my second attempt to reach the bothy. Some places are elusive and take more than one try. My first attempt was foiled by deep snow and I had to take refuge in a mountain emergency shelter. That was in February; now it's four weeks later. Not only has the snow melted but now the days are longer and I can walk into the evening. I'm glad of that extra daylight – last month I would have been in darkness by now, and a remote, unfamiliar Highland glen is a lonely place in the depths of a winter's night.

Slowly, very slowly, the little isolated bothy draws closer. At last, weary and cold, I push open the wind-scoured bothy door. Faindouran is a modest place. There is only one room with a platform to sleep on, a table, a chair and – most important of all – a multi-fuel stove to heat the place. In contrast to its spartan appearance, it boasts one of the most elaborate candelabra I've ever seen in a bothy. It's a multi-branched thing that wouldn't be out of place in the most elegant of dining rooms, yet here it sits in a humble bothy. Perhaps it committed some terrible sin in a past life and now must live the life of a hermit in this remote hut.

Now I have reached the bothy I want to do everything at

once.

I want to:

Have a meal

Have a whisky

Light the fire

Fetch water

Take my boots off

Have a whisky (did I mention that?)

All these activities jostle for priority like greedy children at a Christmas party: I want everything and I want it now! I settle into a well-rehearsed routine. The first thing is to find water. Once I have enough water for the evening I won't have to leave the bothy again and I can take these damned heavy boots off. I find a stream close by, then I have a little whisky – I think I've earned that.

I light the fire, set up my little gas stove and cook my evening meal. 'Cook' is a slight exaggeration. I heat my tin of stewed steak and mix my dehydrated mashed potato with boiled water. The hot food rouses my sleeping appetite. Suddenly I am ravenous and devour the meal in seconds.

I have gazed into the embers of a great many bothy fires in my time. No two are the same. Each fire has its own personality. Some roar into life at the touch of a match flame and have you backing away as the heat sears your eyebrows. Others must be coaxed into life and then smoulder with all the enthusiasm of a Klu Klux Klan member visiting Soweto. This fire was recently installed and is a small cast-iron affair with a splendid gleaming stainless-steel chimney. Faindouran lay semi-derelict for many years after the gable end blew down in a fierce storm several years ago. I am very grateful I wasn't in the bothy that night. The bothy was rebuilt not long ago by the Mountain Bothies Association, although it remained fireless for over a year.

In winter I won't go near a bothy that doesn't have a fire – no fire, no bothy is my mantra. I had avoided heading in to Faindouran until I heard that the Association had installed some heating. I still had to carry my coal all the way in but now it's cheerfully burning in the little black box I can sit back, relax and watch the 'bothy TV'.

There is only one problem. Whilst the coal is burning heartily, the little stove seems to have an uncanny ability to hold on to its heat and remains resolutely cold to the touch. I wrap up in my duvet jacket and try to convince myself I am not cold but my breath still mists in the candlelight and leaves me in no doubt of the chill. Despite humping several kilograms of coal across the frozen wastes of the Cairngorms, I am still cold.

Despondent, I snuggle further into my jacket and take another sip of whisky. "If I can't get warm from the outside, I may as well get warm from the inside."

I turn the pages of the bothy book in an effort to pass the time until the fire finally decides to give off a warm glow. Here I make a stunning literary discovery: the book has been added to by a literary genius. A writer who could be placed alongside Shakespeare or Dickens. There is one simple entry I will never forget.

It reads:

'WHAT A FUCKING RELIEF THIS PLACE IS.'

I have written thousands of words about my visits to bothies. I have waxed lyrical about them. Struggled with what little literary ability I have to bring to life for the reader, at home in his or her armchair, what it is like to journey through remote countryside to these simple dwellings. I know now that all my struggles have been in vain, that every word I have written has been wasted. There, in that book, with one simple sentence, the writer has summed up with dazzling lucidity the essence of the bothy experience.

Like a meal for the starving man or a drink of water for one dying of thirst, the bothy rises out of the bog or emerges from the mist at precisely the moment we need it. It saves us from despair, rescues us from howling gales and torrential rain. It is a roof over our heads just at the moment we need it most and brings back our appreciation for the basic things in life. The pain may be self-inflicted but its relief is always sweet. I am humbled by such a great writer.

Just as I finish reading those words in the logbook I realise that the temperature has risen and the little stove is now belting out so much heat I am forced to strip down to my shirtsleeves. Though I burn only half the coal I carried across all those miles, I spend the evening basking in the glory of the little stove. Through this night in the great darkness at the heart of the Cairngorms, my single candle offers the only pinprick of light. How rare it is, on this crowded island, to find such solitude.

The following day, on the way home, I take a gamble and, instead of walking the long way round via the Fords of Avon as I came in, I follow the shorter route over the hill. I don't know what conditions underfoot will be like when I leave the track and, if the ground is rough and boggy, I might find myself struggling to make any headway. I could lose my gamble.

Happily the hill proves good going on this occasion and the shorter route out is much easier. It is, of course, a big help that I'm not carrying a bag of coal. High on the hill I look back down to the little bothy nestling in the glen and wonder when I'll warm my feet at its fire again. Faindouran's remoteness ensures that only two or three folk visit it each month during the winter – and even these few guests can be dissuaded by the harsh Cairngorm weather. It is in the top five most inaccessible bothies. Like many places that are hard won, the rewards of getting there are so much greater, and you are sure to find the little lonely bothy a welcome relief.

Four weeks earlier, the story was very different.

I stand for a few moments, gathering my breath for the next step. The thigh-deep snow holds my legs in a tight grip, like a toddler pleading for sweets. I heave myself out of the cold, wet potholes and take a few steps on the snow. The icy crust holds my weight for a few seconds before it betrays me and I plunge, for the hundredth time, into the icy water beneath. I have travelled four feet since I was last in this position and my rucksack gets heavier with every step. It's taken me ten minutes to move 100 metres. Hope may spring eternal, but it can just as easily turn into despair.

Winters in these islands are fickle. One moment you are buffeted by blizzards and the next warmed by a gentle sun. This year, winter has been even less predictable than usual; in fact, we barely had a winter at all. The *Daily Mail* headlines predicting the worst winter for one hundred years with dire warnings of blizzards – headlines that brought hope to climbers and skiers – never came true. Our hills were only fleetingly graced with white and most of the season remained depressingly black.

I decided that, as there was so little snow and winter had already left the hills, I would head into the heart of the Cairngorms and spend a night in a bothy I long dreamt of, the distant Faindouran. Poring over the map, I realised that the little shelter would be a long walk from any direction. I had set off early that morning, my pack bulging with coal and comforts, full of optimism for the day ahead.

That morning, as I trekked past the Green Lochan and made my way up through the twisted Scots pine, the remnants of the old Caledonian forest, it felt as though spring had arrived early. Even though it was February it was warm in the glen. The high hills were only dotted with odd patches of snow. As I left the narrow cleft of the glen and walked on beyond to where Ryvoan bothy sits, huddled at the foot of the hill, I stepped out into the vast rolling landscape that leads into the heart of these mountains. I have been coming to the Cairngorms for over forty years, but their scale always surprises me. My eyes took in miles of open country in one sweep: great expanses of heather topped, here and there, by rocky outcrops rounded by millennia of wind and rain.

It is a long climb over the shoulder of the mountain, Bynack More. I was grateful when I reached its rounded crest and began the descent into the Fords of Avon basin, the true heart of the Cairngorm mountains. I was relaxed, if a little leg weary, and already looking forward to warming myself beside the small bothy stove at the end of the day.

It was here, as I approached the Fords of Avon, where the great glens of the Cairngorms converge, that winter ambushed me.

* * *

My pack feels much heavier now and great banks of snow sweep down from the surrounding hills. Despite the warmth of the day, the river is covered in sheets of thick ice. This is where winter has been hiding, waiting for me to bumble over the horizon. At first, I fight my way down through the deep snow into the glen, telling myself that the snow will be thinner lower down and the going easier. Now I have reached the glen I can see that the snow is even deeper and the going harder.

The little stove in Faindouran seems a long way off as I am overtaken by the growing realisation that I no longer have the strength to walk out the way I came in. As I approach the Fords of Avon where the great glens converge, and ominous clouds begin to loom over the mountains around me, I realise I'm not going to make the bothy. Increasingly I feel alone and vulnerable in this vast place. To my right is Loch Avon, its grey waters surrounded by towering cliffs as it sits beneath Cairn Gorm with its wind-scoured summit. Ahead of me the glen leads to the south, to Derry Lodge and ultimately Braemar. To my left another glen heads for Tomintoul, many miles away. Faindouran sits in this glen but it is over four miles away and I doubt I am making one mile per hour in this frozen soup. Already the light is fading, storm clouds are gathering, and my situation is growing serious. Without shelter, I face the prospect of a long cold night – at best. My brain searches for a solution.

Then I remember the Fords of Avon refuge, a little emergency shelter that must be close by. The last time I visited the place it was during a search with the rescue team. It wasn't much more than a metal box resembling a dog kennel. I recall opening the door and finding the floor running with water. A night in that cold place does not have much appeal but I realise I am rapidly running out of both energy and options.

From somewhere in my head an image appears: someone called Neil drinking beer in a newly renovated bothy. It's possible that the place I am remembering is the refuge, so maybe it's been renovated. It's hard to be sure because there are lots of photos of someone called Neil drinking beer in bothies.

The refuge is very close now; it's been close for a long time, so tortuously slow is my progress. At last I stand beside the refuge and it *has* been renovated! The metal box is gone and has been replaced by what looks like a garden shed, heavily insulated, with rocks piled around it. Inside the floor is dry, there is no furniture and I can barely stand, but at least I am out of the weather.

Thud! I crack my head on a low beam. This place has been cleverly designed. It must have taken them ages to get the beams at exactly the right height to collide with the top of my skull. Thud! As I stagger about from one concussive impact to the next I realise that the beams are here to teach me a lesson.

Thud! *You are an old man and should be at home watching Countdown.*

Thud! *You should have known there would be snow here.*

Thud! *Your days of running about the hills are over.*

My candle flame burns undisturbed while wind and rain

hammer at the shelter, a testimony to how weatherproof this place is. In my duvet jacket I am remarkably comfortable. With little else to do I while away the hours reading the graffiti on the wooden walls. Why is it people feel the need to mark their passage by scribbling on things? The Mountain Bothies Association even provides a book and a pen so you can let us know you were here, but that's not good enough; people feel they have to mark the place with names and dates.

A party from Harrogate once had lunch here, and some bloke called Ken from Manchester is a regular visitor. Zoe Partington leaves nothing more than her name. I wonder who she is and what brought her to this remote spot.

I pass the night in the little shelter, dwarfed by Cairngorm giants and alone in the darkness. As I sit dozing, sipping my whisky, I raise a glass to the people who renovated this tiny haven; for without it and their efforts, I would have struggled through a harsh night and perhaps I wouldn't have seen the dawn. The Fords of Avon refuge was not built to be just another bothy. This place was not put here for Zoe to eat her sandwiches in. This place was built to save the lives of the unlucky and the foolish, of which I am both. This place was built for nights like this.

To be read in a Welsh accent.

Zoe Partington, love of my life,
Lips like ripe cherries, breasts of delight
Eyes like stars.
Marry me Zoe Partington, marry me.

She never would say yes but she never did say no.
Years later I met her in Asda, children in tow.
Married the butcher in Cardiff Street see.
I asked her, Zoe why him why not me?
She thought for a while and then she said.
'Well he had more meat.'

Now you can't argue with that can you.

Are You A Real Man?

The wind rattles the bothy door and pushes hopefully against the window panes. The frames flex under the pressure of the gale but I know they'll hold and I let myself relax with my tea. There's nothing like a cup of tea in a bothy; the humble everyday brew is transformed into heavenly nectar.

It's early evening in Bearnais bothy, a remote west-coast shelter not too distant from the village of Lochcarron. Bearnais is a long walk from anywhere. The path is difficult to follow as it winds its way in an odd diagonal up from the coast before it crosses the high ridge at over 2,000 ft to descend into the broad and silent glen. I savour a mouthful of the hot tea, rubbing my aching legs and enjoying the steam rising from the dark liquid. I am pretending to read a book, but each time I read a paragraph my eyelids begin to droop and I find myself dreaming of snow-covered peaks and endless open landscapes instead. Jerking awake, I almost overturn my mug, and when I look down at the beverage I notice something floating on its surface. It's a mouse turd.

I sit for a moment, staring at this unwanted visitor to my beverage, hoping it will magically transform into something a little more welcome – a seed perhaps, a fragment of biscuit – but no, it stares back at me and is, unmistakably, mouse crap. I fish it out with a spoon and I'm then faced with a dilemma, what to do with the tea. I was enjoying it a moment ago, revelling in the taste, but now it appears slightly less appetising. Option one is to throw the tea away and start again. Option two is to man up and finish the tea and pretend nothing has happened. After all, won't it taste just as good as it did before?

* * *

Look up the word 'bothy' in a dictionary and it will tell you it is a simple mountain shelter. These buildings are found in many remote places across Scotland and vary from basic one-room survival shelters to whole cottages boasting flushing toilets; but there is much more to a night in a bothy than just a place to rest your head.

These basic shelters, devoid of electricity or even rudimentary plumbing in most cases, are surrounded by myth and legend. Some of these remote places have worldwide fame whilst others, even in this age of the information superhighway, are kept secret by a devoted few who only whisper their names on dark, candlelit nights in remote glens. We live in a world full of digital technology, our brains deluged with information and constantly bombarded by sounds and images. The digital age is a wonder – humanity has invented a magic more powerful than any medieval wizard could ever have imagined. We can see things that are not there, talk to people who are thousands of miles away. We are now more intimately connected to each other than ever before. It is only because of the internet that you can read these words; without modern technology I would never have been published.

But as I set off on the walk in to Bearnais bothy I follow my usual ritual: I turn off my mobile phone, place it in a little plastic bag and stow it in my rucksack. I will not turn it back on again until I return to 'civilisation'.

The track climbs gently out of the tiny village of Lochcarron – there's a station, a few houses and a pub (I'm not sure that even counts as a village). I feel myself relax as I climb, sweating gently under my pack, the cares of the world beginning to slide away. Now I have radio silence the trip has begun, and I am leaving the chatter of the digital age behind. It is not so long ago that telephones sat on the hall table and were connected to the wall by a wire. When I called my father, who was in his ninetieth year, he would always answer '5402' – so rare were phones in his experience that a four-digit code was unique. In contrast I am bound to the real world by innumerable email addresses, sign-in codes, IP addresses and several phone numbers. I am tracked as I move through the landscape, categorised, my shopping habits analysed and sold on to retailers while robots steer me towards products I might like. Then I turn off my phone and in an instant vanish from the radar screen.

"I'll be away for a few days, in a bothy. You won't be able to email me." I'm talking to my publisher.

There is an uncomprehending silence at the other end of the phone. "Okay, I'll text you."

"Er no, that won't work either," I try to explain.

"Messenger?"

"No."

"WhatsApp?"

"Nah, sorry. No connection of any kind."

The grunt at the end of the phone tells me that this idea is heresy. Once, work stopped when you left the office and went home for your tea. Now, in many occupations, there will be a trickle of texts and emails from your boss and underlings well into the night. Not to respond is to show a lack of commitment that will mark you down in your annual appraisal.

It is the joy of bothies that they are, for the most part, beyond the reach of the web and its unrelenting spiders. I dread the time when nowhere in the UK will be beyond the range of a mobile network and we will have lost our wildest places where it is still possible to slip unseen into a world where the evening's passage is marked only by a sinking candle flame. Yet not everyone is keen to enter the underworld of the bothy. I once asked a friend, a committed hillwalker and wild camper, why he never spent a night in a bothy.

He turned to me and said, his voice trembling a little, "Oh, you never know who you'll meet."

There he is right: in these semi-lawless places, there is no way you can govern who your fellow bothy-dwellers will be. In this over-civilised world, the bothy, with its dark, smoke-filled rooms, remains closer to a medieval inn than the cloned, corporate hotels we stay in today.

I meet many different kinds of folk in bothies; the good, the bad and frequently the ugly. Some are escapees like me, others bring the world with them, and others still probably don't know why they are there.

Here are a few of the folk I've met…

The Heavy Goods Vehicles

You will know them by their huge rucksacks that drop to the bothy floor with such velocity that the roof shakes and drizzles dust down on you. Their sacks are crammed with kilos of coal, crates of beer, and vast quantities of sausages, bacon and pork pies. They come from somewhere in Scotland – no one really knows where, for their language is incomprehensible to anyone who lives more than five miles from their place of birth. Their aim is to raise the temperature in the bothy to the same level as the surface of the sun. Only then can beer and whisky be consumed in sufficient quantities to liberate the 'Craic'. The 'Craic' (pronounced *crack*) is an alcohol-induced ritual where the winner is the person who produces the most creative insults for the assembled company.

Despite their ferocious appearance, and the aggressive grunts with which they communicate, they are friendly. The only exception to their good nature is if you were to deliberately damage one of their beloved bothies, in which case you'd better be able to run because they will hunt you down with a terrible vengeance in their hearts.

The Bothy Ticker

Late at night, when everyone else is sleeping, you will see them indulge their guilty pleasure. Hands quivering with excitement, they seek out the precious list from the bottom of their rucksack and tick off their latest achievement. They've done all the Munros, the Corbetts and the Grahams but their addiction to lists drives them on relentlessly. Without a long list of places to visit, their life is bereft of meaning and so they turn to ticking off bothies. But look into their eyes when they are distracted for a moment. There is a sadness there, born of an awful fear, for every ticker knows that the list always ends. They dread the final tick and know that when the list is done they will feel again that awful, empty yearning. It is then their endless quest begins again, and they must seek another list until, at last, it is they that are ticked.

The Pilgrim

I come to bothies to leave the world behind, others come for solitude, but the Pilgrim searches for that most elusive thing of all: he seeks to find himself. He wanders the lonely glens and moors, crosses high hills and raging rivers, endures the bite of the midge and the sting of the tick. He suffers all these things so that he might better know himself, thinking always that truth lies over the next horizon or behind the bothy door. You will know him by his restless eyes that forever seek things unseen, that search the darkest corners of the world for the secrets of life. The tragedy of the Pilgrim is that he never learns that all his wanderings are in vain. For the thing he seeks is inner peace, and that has been with him all the time.

The Poet

Something odd happens to people in bothies. Deprived of TV and the opportunity to watch barely recognisable celebrities competing on the dance floor, deprived of hours wandering the corridors of the internet, some people feel the urge to put their thoughts into verse. Bothy logbooks are full of dreadful odes to wandering across the hills pursued by midges, often accompanied by illuminating illustrations no one would normally own up to in polite society. The evils of TV and the web are much alluded to but if without them we would be subjected to voluminous outpourings of barely literate adolescent drivel then all the technology we watch clearly has an important role to play. If TV prevents poetry, then it should be provided free everywhere.

The Disappointed

In the 1970s a group of German hikers strolled into the Cairngorms and headed for the Fords of Avon refuge, which they could clearly see on the map. They carried with them nothing but waterproofs and cash, planning to pay for an evening meal and a bed for the night. No doubt they expected a cordial welcome from the resident warden and his team of cooks and housemaids, expecting a continental-style alpine hut. What greeted them was a coffin-like box in which four people could spend the night, provided they knew each other very well and didn't mind spending eight sleepless hours with their knees folded under their chins. A long and very uncomfortable night followed.

Such folk still visit bothies, expecting hotel-style accommodation, and are filled with horror when they ask where the bathroom is only to be handed a spade. You will find them searching the walls for the electric plug sockets and they always leave at first light, heading for the nearest place where their credit cards can be used.

The Veteran

You can spot the Veteran by the way he sits and scowls beside the bothy fire. His equipment is ancient and faded, and he gives off a peculiar pungent smell of damp clothes and rotting socks. The Veteran has been everywhere and done everything. In his day, miles were longer, mountains higher, and rock faces steeper. The Veteran climbed in halcyon days and always looks back to a time when the hills were wild and free, and your wife couldn't phone you when you were on the hills. The Veteran has been doing this since he was a boy. Boots were stout and hearts were bold when he started walking. The trouble with remembering a golden age is that everything else seems dull by comparison; nostalgia sees with rose-tinted glasses.

The Bushcraft Expert

This type of bothy dweller is becoming much more common in the British Isles. Once mainly a European migrant and seasonal visitor, they are now seen further north, possibly the result of climate change. Mostly they have limited experience of the outdoors but may have been on a course that taught them how to survive on berries and make fire by rubbing sticks. They spend their days worrying about the carbon footprint of their times in the wilds. For this reason they gather a few twigs together and sit shivering over a meagre fire whilst they stir tepid water into their five grams of couscous. Their gurus are folk like Ray Mears who they see on their TV screens sitting in a remote forest fashioning an Aga from a few deer teeth and the heel of an old Wellington boot. Mears shows them an ancient way of lighting a fire by using the sparks generated from the static of a nylon pullover. This technique was handed down to him by his forefathers. My dad showed me how to light a fire; he used matches and fire lighters easily obtainable from places called shops. Matches work a treat, Mr Mears.

The Gear Freak

This type of bothy dweller always has the latest equipment. His waterproofs are always dry for they are far too expensive for him to take out in the rain. Given the opportunity he will tell you that you are wearing the wrong socks and how inadequate your jacket is. He can wax lyrical for hours over the benefits of different types of stove, explain the intricacies of head torch components and drone on for an eternity about which is the best fork to eat packet noodles with. Oddly he and the Veteran are good companions as they argue late into the night about the pros and cons of modern gear, neither willing to concede a point until the other is exhausted or dawn breaks.

The Ghillie (an ancient Highland word meaning 'He who strangles deer for a posh bloke in a helicopter')

You'll never find these men in a bothy because Ghillies have an unparalleled understanding of the outdoors. They know that the outdoors is best kept where it should be, outside a door or a window. The Ghillie is a man who has discovered something wonderful: central heating. He has no wish to go near anything cold or wet or remotely natural or unpleasant unless he is paid to do so. He sometimes visits bothies but only to get out of the rain or avoid the midges. He will tolerate the collection of halfwits – as he regards anyone who voluntarily goes outdoors – that he finds in the bothy, because it's been carefully explained to him that shooting them is illegal. As soon as the rain eases off he steps out of the bothy to find something natural and kill it. Then he goes home to his house, where it's warm and dry and there's none of that awful weather stuff.

The Pontificator

The last on our list of people you are likely to stumble over in bothies is the most odious of them all. The Pontificator is normally a solitary animal but in the small group of folk huddled round the bothy fire he finds what he craves most of all, an audience. Fuelled by whisky he will expound his views to all those captive in this crude shelter. He is keen to tell anyone and everyone about his views on bothies and the outdoors. Sometimes, sadly, his ramblings get published on websites and in books about hillwalking, further inflaming the ego of this crushing bore.

* * *

I stare down into my tea still trying to decide if I should drink it. In all my bothy ramblings, I must have consumed a fair bit of mouse crap and I appear to be in robust health most of the time. Indeed, there are certain foodstuffs that even today have permitted levels of mouse crap in them. Rice is one of them.

If a waiter were to ask you, "How much mouse excrement would you like to take with your curry today, sir?" it's hard to think just how much might be acceptable. Perhaps, however, we have become a little too squeamish in association with our rodent brethren. In medieval times people must have lived in homes infested with the little souls and, due to the lack of dishwashers, eaten rather a lot of the stuff. Our obsession with living in sterile environments is a relatively modern notion.

So drinking mouse-soiled tea is hardly likely to kill me? There are things I wouldn't like to do though. I read recently that a man had to have a tape worm removed from his brain. Apparently, it got into his head after he was treated by a Chinese apothecary using raw frog. I'm not sure what he was being treated for but if the cure is having a tape worm in your brain it must have been pretty nasty. In the end, I man up and drink the tea.

Wandering out from the bothy the following day I felt no ill effects although hopefully that's not because the worm in my brain had affected my judgement. Who knows, perhaps it's controlling me as I write now.

I know as I write this that one of the HGVs described above will read this incredulously.

"Wit, wit? He fished it oot! Ah cannae ken wha's the wrang wi the man, is he some kind aw jessie?"

I'll translate: "What? He removed the mouse faeces from his tea! I don't understand what's wrong with the man, does he have some sort of genetic weakness?"

Better stop now, feeling a bit queasy.

The Unforgiven Mountaineer

"Actually, I'm not a Munroist."

The words cut through the air like pieces of shrapnel. Suddenly everyone falls silent. No one dares move.

* * *

Invermallie bothy sits on the shores of Loch Arkaig only a few miles from where that enormous stretch of water spews into the River Arkaig and heads for the Great Glen. Its proximity to the water is both its charm and its downfall. I had enjoyed the walk in along the edge of the loch, strolling along the little track beside the water's edge and catching glimpses of the waves rolling across the surface. It's October now and the trees are still green with leaves; soon autumnal gales will rake across the glens, stripping the branches of their golden colours. Today, fortunately, those tempests are yet to arrive and only a gentle breeze ripples the surface of the loch. I am used to the long hard slogs of many a Highland bothy, so I feel at ease as I find myself walking into the small, wooded glen that is home to Invermallie, knowing I have not far to go.

It is then that I learn the downside of the bothy's proximity to the loch. Large sections of the track are underwater, and I'm forced to pick a difficult, complex route between pools, over branches and along the sides of ruts in the track. At last I arrive

– miraculously with dry feet – at the bothy. It is typical of so many: a low stone building with a central porch that houses the only door, and a window either side for the two downstairs rooms. There is a small lean-to firewood shelter at one end of the building and, ominously, what appears to be a watermark about three feet up the stone walls. It looks as though this little bothy is no stranger to flooding and, although the rain ceased earlier this morning, the mountain streams are still in spate and thousands of gallons of water are heading for the loch. It occurs to me that there is a real chance of becoming marooned here.

Inside the bothy I can hear muffled voices and, as my eyes adjust to the gloom, I discern three figures clustered around the bothy fire. Rick is a large, slightly overweight retired teacher from Kent. Steve, a bearded, wizened elf of a man, is a postman. The third introduces himself as David and looks every inch an English gent but speaks with a hint of an Irish accent. They seem pleased to see me and explain that they are all members of the same mountaineering club in the south of England.

"Will you not take some tea?" David asks, and soon my mug is full of a steaming brew.

The bothy is festooned with wet clothes. Trousers hang from an intricate string system on the ceiling, while socks take pride of place above the smouldering fire and drip merrily onto the wooden floor. The air is filled with the reek of woodsmoke and the smell of sweat. In other words, it smells like every bothy I've ever been in.

Looking around the bothy I spot other telltale signs. There is a map open on the table. It has summits ringed and linked by little lines of biro. Some have ticks and others do not. I know instantly what these men are: they are followers of a different god, they are Munroists.

If you have been fortunate enough never to have heard of such folk then let me explain the origin of their affliction. A Victorian gentleman called Sir Hugh Munro, having little better to do, decided to count all the mountains in Scotland over 3,000 feet. At the time there were believed to be around 30 such peaks, but Sir Hugh discovered, much to everyone's astonishment, that there are closer to 270. Sadly the curious aristocrat then compiled a list of these peaks. These days, a great many folk, unable to explore the hills on their own initiative, slavishly follow Sir Hugh's list and are thus known as Munroists. Their aim is to climb every hill on the list. The more seriously afflicted continue to climb other lists completed by people also of an obsessive or compulsive disposition – lists such as the Corbetts and Donalds.

"Terrible weather," David says, staring into his tea.

Rick struggles to get his bulk comfortable on the narrow wooden bench. "We've been out two days and got soaked to the skin on both of them."

"Aye, soaked," they chorus.

I wait for the question, but it doesn't come, and I wonder if I'll get lucky this time.

As the evening progresses we gradually begin to get to know each other. The three walkers ask me for tips about local bothies and I'm happy to give them what information I can. Tins of beer are produced. I share some whisky and a happy convivial atmosphere develops.

Then Rick turns to me, a little mellowed by the whisky. "So, how many have you done?"

I pretend I haven't heard him, but he repeats the question and I feel a tension form in the room. Sometimes I think it would be so much easier to lie, to pick a number out of the air and cling to it as my life raft in a sea of despair. Then they'd smile and nod knowingly, happily content that I was one of them, a fellow traveller in their man-made topographical quest.

"I've only 27 left to do," I could say and everyone would grin, confident I was one of the brethren and we could relax and talk about boots and rucksacks and how bad the midges were. I could do that, but I don't. I swallow my whisky and utter the heresy.

"Actually, I'm not a Munroist."

* * *

My words hang in the air like a malevolent fart. No one speaks, and we are all suddenly aware of the drip, drip of the saturated socks onto the bothy floor. I suck on my whisky and stare as hard as I can into the bothy fire. Perhaps I'll see a genie in the flames who'll whisk me away from the coming confrontation. Tearing my eyes from the flickering flames I peer through the gloom and steaming socks at the other three men.

Rick, struggling to find a response to my answer, is twisting his grey whiskers to a point with a vehemence that threatens to tear the hair from his face. David giggles nervously. I know what he's thinking. He's trying to figure out, if it comes to it, and he lunges for his ice axe hanging over the fire, will I get there first?

Rick emits an odd gurgle and then manages to twist it into

the beginning of a sentence: "Yes… but…"

David lets out a short titter, or perhaps it's a sob. If we were in a Western saloon, instead of a rain-soaked bothy on the west coast of Scotland, at this point the piano would fall silent, everyone would have stopped playing cards and the barman would be reaching for a hidden shotgun.

"Yes but… you must at least know how many." Rick is growing desperate, as if he can't stop turning over my words in his mind.

"I've no idea how many hills I've climbed. I don't count them."

I can relax now the words have finally been uttered. The unbeliever is unmasked. There is another reason I feel at ease: I'm not as quick as I used to be but I have worked out the answer to the problem that's been troubling David for the last few minutes. I am closer to the ice axe than he is.

I'd known this point would come – sooner or later, it always does.

Things are always fine until they ask me that question and I reveal that I am the child of a different god. I tell them I despise everything they have spent years trudging over the hills trying to achieve. I prove to them that they have been chasing an illusion all these years, and that nothing is as it seems. I ruin everything.

Rick staggers to the end of his sentence like an old man who has climbed his last hill. "You don't count them! But what's the point of that?" I see his eyes mist over as he ponders that last statement and realises that there *is* no point.

I feel about as welcome as if I were wearing a white peaked

hood and sitting in the congregation of an African American church in Alabama. I've long since stopped trying to explain; I've come to realise that it must be me that doesn't understand. I am the odd one out not them. I think of the hills as a rare oasis of freedom in an otherwise over-regulated desert. Everywhere there are rules about what we must and must not do. The legions of people telling me what I should do are almost cancelled out by the thousands of folk telling me what I shouldn't. I thought I could escape all this in the hills – go where I pleased, sit and look at the view if I felt like it or just wander aimlessly – but no, it seems I've been getting it all wrong.

Perhaps human beings have a yearning to be regulated, sorted, categorised and numbered. Just when we found somewhere to escape to that was not stamped beneath the heel of the corporate logo, and were wondering what to do with all that freedom, salvation came in the form of Sir Hugh waving his list. Imagine the relief: no longer would hillwalkers have to walk aimlessly in the hills, now there was someone who had found the piece of paper that tells us all what to do and where to go. Thank God we're saved!

In the words of Patrick McGoohan's character, Number Six, in *The Prisoner*: "I am not a number, I am a free man!"

Back in the bothy, I make a lunge for the ice axe.

The Night The Bothy Burned

Even though it is mid-July the bothy is cold and damp. Pete sits stroking his ginger beard, his large frame squeezed into a folding chair, as I arrange a few sticks in the fireplace. Satisfied with the arrangement I turn to pick up the matches.

"Hello," he says. "Where did you come from?"

There is only him and me in the little stone cottage of Gleann Dubh-Lighe, so I can't understand whom he is talking to. Then I look down to see a mouse sitting in the fireplace, gazing back at Pete. The mouse looks at ease with us and doesn't seem at all concerned at the presence of two visitors. Pete – who always has food about his person – produces a small pork pie from the folds of his jacket and hurls a crumb to the mouse. The little creature darts forward and collects the crumb, which is nearly the size of its head, and vanishes back into the fireplace.

I sit down beside Pete, matches in my hands. "I think we just paid the rent."

Pete sighs. "Tame, wasn't he? Must get fed by everyone who comes here."

We can't light the fire now without risking cooking the mouse, so the rest of the evening passes without the warmth of the fire.

* * *

The following day we climbed the hill behind the bothy, Streap, so that poor Pete (a sufferer from the Munro addiction) could cross it off his list of Corbetts. That night with Pete and the bold mouse was over 30 years ago. In the intervening time I have wandered through many Highland glens and spent over half my life in Scotland, yet still there are so many hills I have not climbed and glens I have not walked through.

There is a common misconception that the world has become a smaller place now that we can all jump on a jet plane and travel halfway around the globe. In contrast, I am always amazed at how large the Highlands are. I have spent the greater part of my life here and yet there are so many places I have not seen. In recent years I have become increasingly fascinated by the vast, wild and empty area known as Sutherland. This northern county of the Highlands is so huge I could probably spend the rest of my life exploring there and not see the whole place. Sutherland covers an area of over 2,000 square miles, which should be enough for anyone to walk in. Its size, coupled with the fact that there are few other people there, gives it a unique sense of remoteness. The population is limited to around 12,000, most of whom live in or around the villages of Dornoch and Golspie.

Much of Sutherland might be described as trackless waste by those less romantically inclined than myself. If you are looking for miles and miles of nothing you'll find shedloads of it there. It was widely settled by the Vikings, whose Norse names are everywhere on the map. The area suffered badly during the Clearances, a time when landowners forcibly evicted many families from the Highlands so that they could graze sheep. During that period it's thought that over 1,600 families were forced to leave. Many areas of the Highlands never recovered from this population depletion. It's a sad fact that many of the remote and empty areas I enjoy are only the way they are because of the suffering wrought on the population from 300 years ago until late in the 19th century.

I've heard it said that when you are a child time passes in a trickle, and by the time you are an adult it has become a waterfall. So it was with amazement that I realised almost thirty years had passed since I visited the little bothy in the forest. Keen to revisit the spot, I set out once more to spend an evening there. My memories of the place were vague, but I recall it being surrounded by trees and so sheltered by the forest that the air around the little building remained wet and made the place cold and damp.

My fist visit was in July but it was mid-February when I drove down the road to Mallaig that is romantically named 'The Road to the Isles'. It was early evening and almost dark by the time I set off along the track in to the bothy. Fortunately Gleann Dubh-Lighe is only a few miles into the forest and so I knew I should be there with about an hour's walk. Even in daylight every forest track looks much the same as any other and at night they are all indistinguishable. I have learned, from bitter experience, that it is vital to make sure that you are setting out along the right route; once in the woods, you'll be staring at thousands of identical pine trees. More than once I've chosen the wrong track and spent a frustrating time walking down the wrong glen. That's a navigational error that is surprisingly easy to make.

Peter Cliff, who was Team Leader when I joined the Cairngorm Mountain Rescue team, wrote the bible on finding your way about the hills: an invaluable little book called *Mountain Navigation*. Peter once told me that the most common error is to simply have the compass the wrong way around and thus set off 180 degress in the wrong direction.

There is a moon tonight but its great shining face is obscured by the trees and I am following the small pool of light my head torch casts on the ground. I'm confident I am precisely where I should be but I am relieved when the little bridge over the river (which I know is close to the bothy) appears on cue, exactly where I thought it would be. The bridge is sheathed in ice and sparkles in my torch light as I begin to cross. The ice on the polished wood has made the surface treacherous and I can hear the river roaring as I cautiously make my way across, acutely aware of the torrent below. There is a handrail on one side of the bridge so I cling tightly to that as I inch forward. In the daylight I would stroll casually across what is little more than a stream but the darkness adds an extra degree of menace to the situation. I shuffle forward, my torch fixed on my feet, as I definitely do not want to find myself stepping into the space left by a missing plank. It is at this point that my fingers slip from the handrail and I find myself grabbing at empty space. I look up for the handrail and it has vanished; off balance, my feet slide away, and I fall face down onto the icy wooden planks of the bridge. Looking up I see what I had not noticed before: a large section of the handrail is missing. I had been so focused on my feet I hadn't seen this and had nearly been pitched into the torrent.

Glad that my ribs have been dented less than my pride, I make the far side of the bridge with little further difficulty. Now I begin counting steps to ensure I don't miss the bothy. Most bothies are made of local stone and, in the darkness, they have an unfortunate habit of blending chameleon-like into their backgrounds. Step-counting is a dark art. The distance you cover with each step varies with the terrain, how much weight you are carrying, and – often – how much you had to drink the previous evening.

"969, 970. Perhaps I'd better start looking for the bothy now."

I lift my head and the gable end of Gleann Dubh-Lighe appears in my torch beam. The gods of step-counting are smiling upon me tonight; perhaps they took pity on me after watching me fall flat on my face crossing the bridge.

A warm glow of candlelight illuminates the bothy windows and I'm curious to see who I'll be spending the evening with. The interior has been transformed from my memory of it. The dull, dusty, wood-lined walls are gone; now the walls gleam, the wood varnished with a gloss that reflects the light of the fire and the candles. A rare thing in a bothy. The little mouse that greeted us so cheekily on my last visit must have been eating cheese in mouse heaven for many years, the ancient ancestor to any current rodent occupiers.

The occupants of the bothy are a young, slim, dark-haired woman and a slightly older man with weather-beaten features and a grizzled beard. The woman is feathering wood for the fire, the blade of her knife glinting in the candlelight, and the man is busying himself cooking. They greet me warmly and soon we are chatting about bothies we have been to and the characters we've met in our travels.

"I hear this place burnt down a few years ago. How could some fool burn down a bothy?" I ask, more to pass the time than out of any real curiosity.

The woman freezes when I asked the question. She's tall and dark, her features even and sharp with the dark-haired beauty Irish women sometimes have. Her companion catches my eye and shakes his head.

"I don't think there's any need to ask about things like that."

For a few moments we all sit in silence, staring into the flames of the fire. Then the woman begins carving again and we all watch how the steel blade cuts deep into the wood.

"It's a fair question," she murmurs at last, more to herself than to us. Then she looks me in the eye and I feel my blood run cold. "How *does* some fool burn down a bothy?" she adds.

The bearded man puts his hand on her shoulder as if to silence her but she pushes him away.

"That's a good question, maybe it deserves an answer." She pauses, and we wait as she struggles to find the words. "It might have been a candle left unguarded, or perhaps a log from the fire or a gas stove knocked over – it could have been any of those things." She tosses the stick she has been working on into the fire. The flames devour it greedily, bringing a burst of light to the bothy. "But it wasn't any of those things."

I can see now how she is struggling to contain her emotions, how something deep and dark within tortures her mind. There are tears in her eyes and I want to return the demon I have released to the cage she holds it in.

"Please, I don't need to know," I stammer, but the demon

would not be denied.

She looks down at the knife in her hand and then quickly back at me and the anger in her eyes startles me.

“Have you ever been in love? I mean really in love, consumed by it. So you can’t eat, you can’t sleep, so all you think about, day and night, is them.”

She falls silent again and I can see that she has travelled to some distant place in her mind.

“We were in love, Davy and me, and happy together. One day he told me he was coming to this bothy for a night of peace and quiet. It was a dark November night, the wind rising and hurling the fallen leaves up into the dark night sky as I walked up the glen. I wanted to surprise him, you see. I had a bottle of wine, some bread, a bit of cheese. You know.”

I did know. Simple pleasures in a simple place, good company, peace, with the one you loved. The picture is already in my mind.

“I could see the candlelight in the window,” she says, her voice quivering, “and I pressed my face against the window. I remember the glass, cold.”

She falls silent again and we wait silently, knowing that the tale she was telling could not be stopped.

“They were in here together. Mary worked in the post office. Nice girl. They were cuddling together in front of the fire, laughing. They stopped laughing when I walked in.” She turns, picks up her cup and gulps down her whisky. Then she looks around the room as though she is trying to relive what happened. “I can’t remember what happened then. I shouted, I know that, and I remember him touching me, and me pushing him away." Her companion refills her cup in silence and she drinks again.

"Then I was alone. They ran. I don't blame them." She laughs and for a moment seems younger than her years. "Fire cleanses. I thought that it might stop it hurting and I was angry. A few matches, a little paraffin. You could see the flames from the road they said." That fact seemed to make her proud.

"Oh, I'm sorry," I say, regretting now I'd made her relive that dark night.

"Don't be." She grins, her eyes shining in the candlelight. "He pissed off with a hiker from Glasgow, left Mary with a baby, the wee shite. I was better off without him. Besides we rebuilt the place. Not bad, is it?" She casts her eyes around the bothy, admiring the neatly jointed woodwork. "I came back a few months later to see the scene of the crime. The place was all charred wood. Black and heartless, like me, so I thought I'd rebuild it. Took time and a lot of help but we got the roof on, then the windows in and slowly it came back, became whole again. And as I put it back to how it had been it put me back together as well."

* * *

Sometimes, when I sit looking into a bothy fire, I wonder who has been there over the years. Thousands of walkers must have visited these places over the years and sat, as I do, watching the flames dance around the glowing coals.

Bothies are more than just rough cottages made from cold stone walls. They have a sense of place in our landscape and, for those who visit them, they take root in our imaginations where visits are relived time and time again. They are dwellings where people find peace from the hurly-burly. Many bothies were not always the simple mountain shelters they are today. Once they were shepherds' cottages where children were born, wee families lived out their daily lives and people grew old and died. The folk who lived here must have had hard lives. They coped with the cold and the midges, their children walked long miles to school and returned to cold, dark homes. The women whose jobs it was to keep the fire burning, children clean and food cooked must have had hard lives too, in a continuous battle against the soot from the fire and the icy water they had to draw from the burns.

These bothies have known joy and tragedy. Many have had their own life cycles; built with optimism, they gave folk new homes. Over the years they grew old, were deserted and left cold and dark. Gradually the rain found its way beneath the roof slates, the rafters slowly decayed until, perhaps in some October gale, the roof collapsed, and the timber rotted away until only stone walls remained. But many have been brought back from dereliction, raised from the dead by bodies like the Mountain Bothies Association, and reborn as the mountain shelters we know today.

Listening to her story, I glimpsed one of the past lives of this and the many other bothies I visit. Perhaps the memory of all the lives that have passed through these simple dwellings lives on in the stones. It is reassuring to remember that our lives and the lives of the places we inhabit are inextricable. Nature is within all of us and we are nature. Perhaps this is why we all feel a sense of kinship and brotherhood in bothies.

* * *

When the woman had finished telling her tale we all sit in silence for a moment, not quite knowing how to move on.

"Well," I say at length, "it's a much better place now than it was before the fire."

The woman smiles, and I can see the concept dispelled some of the dark thoughts that had surrounded her.

She looks admiringly around the bothy. "Yes, I think it is a much better place."

"And I'll always be able to say I met the woman who burned down Gleann Dubh-Lighe."

Dry Man Walking

I've been walking this forestry road for the last half hour, kicking my way along the forestry track as fast as I can go. Poles thumping into the dirt, breathing hard, sweating and wondering if I'll get there in time. I'm not sure if I'm going to make it. This is a race and the stakes are high. I can see the rain coming in as a great curtain of grey sweeps towards me down the glen.

At last I emerge from the forest and all around me there is devastation. Trees lie shattered – limbs splintered, branches broken and twisted, a scene of carnage as though some huge battle was fought here and the spent protagonists left only minutes ago. The forestry has been harvested, tall trees felled, and the landscape changed dramatically in only a couple of weeks. The tracks are churned to mud by great earth movers and everywhere fragments of trees lie shattered. There is no escaping the fact that the great serried ranks of trees must be harvested but I never get used to seeing the debris of the aftermath. Soon the machines will return and cover the landscape with young trees to await the return of the forest.

Nowhere I walk – apart from the very summits of the hills, where little can ever grow – is a natural landscape. The hand of man is written everywhere. The great native forests that once covered the Highlands are long gone and have been replaced by open grassland, kept clear by sheep and huge numbers of red deer, or the industrial plantations of trees. Britain has no true wilderness; nowhere is more than a day's walk from a road or a dwelling. Nature, like beauty, is in the eye of the beholder and I find myself increasingly seeking out what I describe as *wildness* as opposed to wilderness.

Wildness is a glimpse of a barn owl leaving its roost on a cold winter's day to make the most of the waning light. Wildness is the flash of white as a stoat darts for cover high on the moors. It is a moment or two watching an otter fishing in the waters of Loch Dubh. It is the wind whispering through the long grass beside the bothy door as the sun sinks and the light of day fades into evening. These things are the same as they were 10,000 years ago and 10,000 years before that. They are primal, they are part of us, they are where we came from and to where we will return. We do not visit nature; we *are* nature.

I am able to visit the wilder parts of Britain and enjoy the remoteness that the Highlands have to offer, but there are glimpses of wildness even in our most urban environments. Anywhere that you can get close to a tree has to be a good place to be. The health benefits of owning a cat or dog are well known. Contact with a cat can lower blood pressure and the need to regularly exercise a dog is likely to increase your fitness and decrease your weight. Perhaps, however, the real benefit of being close to a dog or cat is not in the physical changes they bring – it resides in a need within us all to be close to an animal or at least something natural in our environment. How many people live their entire lives without being able to step off tarmac or concrete and feel the earth beneath their feet? Surely this is something that must be as dangerous to health as stress or the pollutants around us?

* * *

Freed from its shroud of trees, the track leads on into open space where the river meanders lazily in the boggy floor of the glen. I can see Glen Pean bothy now, only half a mile away, the small stone building nestling against the side of the glen just above the flood plain of the river. Beyond the bothy, the green hills steepen and the glen narrows enticing you onwards. The path runs on to Oban bothy beyond where the glen narrows to a sharp 'V'. I've never visited Oban, and the bothy is locked until February. The rumours say it's a little gem of a place, remote and beautiful and only recently open to the public. I file that information away for an adventure in March.

That's a dream for the future; it's today's adventure that holds my attention. The sky is dark and huge black rainclouds lurk behind the outlines of the hills crowding the end of the glen. Beyond the bothy – and approaching fast – is a curtain of grey rain that's been heading my way for a while now. This rain has given my steps urgency through the broken forest. My mind is set on one thing: getting to the bothy before the rain gets to me.

* * *

I have an aversion to rain. I treat it as if it were liquid acid that will strip my body of flesh in minutes. I play cat and mouse with it, timing my walks with precision to dodge the raindrops. The rain knows this. It tries to fool me, luring me out from shelter with little shafts of sunshine, encouraging me to stray into the open where it can pummel me with airborne oceans.

The ancient Gore-Tex jacket I own has long since given up the struggle to hold back the bombardments of water that lurk in the Highlands. It's so old the last time it got wet the tapes on the seams all came loose and left me looking like a soggy Christmas tree. I like the snow, love the cold and can tolerate the wind, but rain is as welcome as a rattlesnake in a lucky dip. I've been wet before and I didn't enjoy the experience.

I've made a trade. In the exchange we all make between time and money I chose time. More simply put, I took early retirement – so I have plenty of time, but not a lot of cash. So far, it's been a good trade. I delight in the freedom. I don't have to get up every morning and talk to people I don't like about things I don't care about. I don't have waste days, looking out of the window, sitting in meetings the outcome of which are of no consequence. I can climb in my car beside the River Ness any time I like, and head for wildness. The freedom I have is worth the occasional soaking; I'll trade new rain gear for this day of freedom. As long as I can make the bothy before the rain gets here, that is.

Glen Pean sits on a thin ribbon of land in line between two great lochs. One is Loch Arkaig, an incredible place. You turn off the main road to Fort William and drive off into a kind of lost world. The loch is huge and the road that runs beside it was designed by Evel Knievel on an off day. It's around fifteen miles of rollercoaster with the added spice of blind bends and oncoming Land Rovers.

Loch Arkaig is to the east but to the west lies an equally spectacular loch, Morar. The loch is over eleven miles long and at over 1,000ft deep it is the deepest body of freshwater in the British Isles, deeper even than the giant, Loch Ness. Its shores are remote and mysterious, and it is even fabled to have its own monster, Morag. Sadly, I am convinced that neither the monster of Loch Ness nor Morag can have any basis in fact. The ecology of neither loch is able to support an animal of that size. Sunlight can only penetrate their waters to a depth of just over a metre, meaning that only seven per cent of the waters are able to sustain life. Having walked and driven along the shores of Loch Ness for many years I can testify to the fact that the geography of the loch – a great deep cleft between long, high hills – does give rise to unusual wave patterns which a fertile imagination can ascribe to the passage of an underwater dinosaur. Unfortunately, it is the wind rather than a monster that creates those waves.

The mystery surrounding Loch Ness is deepened by the fact that the legendary occultist and mountaineer Aleister Crowley once lived in a house on the shore of the loch at a place called Boleskine. Crowley lived there around one hundred years ago at a time when the main road along the lochside ran to the south, through the small village of Dores, not along the north side of the loch as it does today. On market days the farmers of the area would travel to Inverness to sell their produce and return by the evening, inebriated and singing on their empty carts. Crowley, frequently immersed in reading his studies of the occult, grew tired of this disturbance. One night he constructed a fake monster head and waved it above the hedge of his home as the revellers passed. So alarmed were the passers-by that they never again used that route and in future returned home using a considerably longer road.

I have no such monsters to worry about as I head for the door of the little bothy, eyes fixed on the wall of water heading my way. Although the bothy is close, the heavy forestry machinery has ripped the last few hundred yards of track to shreds, so the going is slow as I stumble over the limbs of fallen trees. Eventually, I fall through the bothy door and only moments later the rain arrives and bombards the little bothy with bullets of water. The sound on the tin roof is deafening and I'm grateful to have that barrier between me and the deluge.

If you plan to visit Glen Pean bothy and arrive after dark, take extra care navigating the last few hundred yards. At night these could be very tricky. In the last few hundred yards before the bothy, the path is boggy and indistinct – if it's snowing you might never find it. The bothy is not as obvious as it appears on the map. If you are there in darkness take heart, the only monsters you'll meet are in your own mind.

Of Fire And Men

Towering curtains of rain sweep across the sea loch, dwarfing me and Charlie as we hurry along the small track to the bothy. The walk to Glendubh is only a few miles long, nowhere steep, but it is exposed to the weather as the wild westerly wind sweeps in from the Atlantic.

Charlie turns to me, water dripping off his hat on to his weather-beaten face, and soaking his grey beard. "Occasional showers! That's what the weatherman said, he must have meant that they'd occasionally last most of the bloody day!"

A particularly cold trickle of water finds its way down the back of my neck and I shiver involuntarily. "Not far now, mate." I try to sound cheerful but Charlie doesn't look convinced.

Only the hardiest (or the most stupid) of Highland bothy visitors venture out in November. It may not be the coldest month but its nights are long and dark and its days often filled with endless rain and howling gales. It's only 4.30 but it will be dark in an hour or so. Charlie and I are weighed down with extra coal to survive the hours of darkness. A bothy would be a miserable place at this time of year – especially if you are soaked through to your underwear – without the saving grace of a cheery fire.

At last, through the mist and rain, the outline of the handful of stone cottages appears just as the last of the day's light is fading. The bothy, a small, vacant estate house, and a little storage shed huddle together at the end of the loch where the hills rear up behind them offering some shelter from the westerly wind that rampages in down the valley.

Inside, the air is cold and dank but at least we can enjoy a respite from the deluge outside. Glendubh is a simple place: it has two rooms downstairs and a wooden staircase leading upstairs to two bedrooms nestling in the eaves of the roof. Like many bothies, one room has a decent wooden floor and a good fireplace whilst the other is much more spartan, with only a concrete floor and no fire.

"I'm getting too old for this." Charlie sighs sadly as he examines the saturated lining of his cagoule whilst the water vapour rising from our bodies mists in the torchlight.

I slowly peel off the moist fleece. Now that I'm no longer walking, it feels chill against my skin. "Och, you've a few years yet."

Both of us are in our early sixties and know that our time in the hills may be running out.

Charlie hauls the coal out of his dripping rucksack. "I reckon you'll be coming here in your nineties, but if we stand here much longer we'll freeze to death."

Now Charlie and I have only one thing on our minds: fire. All through that deluge, as our packs grew heavier with rain, one thought kept us going through the drudgery of a wet walk: that once at the bothy we would be able to sit in comfort in front of a roaring fire where we can warm our bones and our soul. There is nothing quite as joyous as sitting safe and warm in a bothy enjoying a dram while a storm rages outside. I always carry a light fleece suit that I bought for around £10 from Lidl or Aldi, which I think the supermarket described as 'leisure wear'. It weighs very little and is perfectly warm and comfortable as long as you never wear it outside the bothy where the elements will rip it to shreds.

The best room in the bothy boasts the remains of what was once a grand Victorian fireplace. The hearth has fallen on hard times now; its grate is cracked and it's many years since a proud housewife blackened the surround until it shone. Today the hearth is choked with ash from previous residents. I'm always amazed at how many folk will leave a bothy with an ash-choked fireplace. Indeed, I often find fireplaces full of the ash from several visits. Sometimes much digging is needed before, like a pyromaniac archaeologist, I unearth the buried fireplace.

In the ash I find bottle tops and beer cans and – what I hate most – the aluminium remains of tealights. Dig in the hearth of any Highland bothy and there they are. They are placed there by folk under the bizarre misapprehension that aluminium burns. Forgive an old man a rant that will only mean something to a small group of bothy dwellers, but I hate tea lights with a vengeance. In their lifetimes, as small candles, they give out precious little light; then, when they are spent, they return in their afterlife to haunt me by blocking up hearths.

Charlie braves the elements and heads outside to empty the ash bucket. I layer coal on the grate, place firelighters then the kindling wood, then another layer of coal. It's a system I've developed over my years with thousands of bothy fires. I light the firelighters and they send gouts of bright yellow flame up the chimney in a joyous conflagration. Charlie and I sit watching the fire.

Until the coal is burning well I'll not take my eye off it; never trust a bothy fire. The firelighters die but the coal is only smouldering, and the kindling is untouched. The wood must be damp since I stored it in my shed, an amateurish mistake. Charlie doesn't say anything but I can see he's not impressed. I kneel before the hearth, like a worshipper at prayer, and huff and puff at the coals, trying to kindle some life – but the flames refuse to rise. For my next trick, I place a newspaper across the hearth to increase the draught. This is a technique my mother used in our Merseyside home when the only source of heating we had in the little semi-detached house was the lounge coal fire. Health and safety hadn't been invented in those days and it was a regular occurrence for the fire to gleefully ignite the paper in my mother's hands whereupon she would casually toss it into the hearth. The newspaper produced no result, and neither did pouring sugar over the fire (my mother did that too). Then I found a metal tube that had once been part of a camp bed, thrust one end into the embers and blew down the other.

"For Christ's sake don't suck." Charlie laughs as he makes one of his evil rollup cigarettes.

Despite my efforts the fire is slowly going out, and the prospect of a long cold night beckons.

* * *

The bothy fire smokes for a few minutes, coughs, splutters and then dies. Charlie stares disconsolately at the cold hearth. "Well that's it then, we've blown on the bloody thing, chucked paraffin on it, tossed everything we can think of and still it won't light. It's going to be a cold night. We've tried every trick."

It's my fault; I left my kindling in the shed and it got damp and won't light. An elementary mistake but a costly one. I've lugged 10 kilos of coal up the track beside the sea and finally dumped it on the floor of Glendubh bothy (pronounced *glendoo*, meaning 'black glen') only to watch it sitting there like a bag of black rocks. Both of us are shivering as we watch our breath misting the air in the candlelight.

Charlie kicks the hearth in frustration. "All that coal and we're still cold. There's nothing else we can do."

I pride myself in being a Fire Master, a veteran of many arctic bothy nights. I can kindle a flame from the coldest, most reluctant hearth, yet this one has defeated me. Lighting a bothy fire is a dark art learnt only through years of patient pyromania. Walking in to a bothy I am always painfully aware of the load of coal crushing into the base of my back. It presses down on you. On hills it holds you back and on descents it pushes you forwards, hurling you downhill in knee-crushing jolts.

"It'll be worth it," I always tell myself, picturing myself toasting my toes before a roaring fire while a storm rages outside. Tonight, that image fades like a mirage and I begin to resign myself to a never-ending frigid evening.

Then suddenly I am back in a thousand dark winter glens; like a Shaolin Kung Fu monk, I have returned, in my moment of crisis, to the temple. I remember all the battles I've had trying to coax fire from reluctant wood. I have blown through tubes, used newspaper to create a draught, prayed, threatened and cajoled fires into life in my many nights of travel. I am the monkey trying to get the orange from the jar, I am the little grasshopper at the feet of the master (you have to be a certain age for that one).

At last, I remember, there is one thing I've not tried on tonight's reluctant fire. A trick I've never used before, an untried technique of firelighting I've held in reserve until now. Charlie watches in mild curiosity as I assemble my gas cooker, carefully attaching the burner to the gas cylinder by the foot-long tube. He's even more fascinated when I remove the front of the fire and push the burner under the grate.

"Oh my god! You can't do that," Charlie, always a man firmly attached to his mortal vessel, exclaims in growing panic.

"Oh, but I can."

I light the gas and the little stove hurls flames up into the cooling coal. I turn to reassure Charlie, but his chair is suddenly empty. I find myself alone in the bothy with only the swinging bothy door to remind me of his passage.

Now, let's just get a few things straight. I've got a stove with a highly flammable gas canister only a few inches from a fire. Some of you will have already passed judgement on the safety of this practice. Others will be undecided. For those of you who have not reached a conclusion, let me quell any doubts. Is this safe? – no. Is it likely to cause permanent injury or even death? – yes.

DO NOT TRY THIS AT HOME!

It is not long before the coal begins to smoke. The stove is doing its job. Looking up, I see a startled expression peering in through the bothy window from the darkness outside. The expression is attached to a face, Charlie's face, with his fingers in his ears.

Suddenly the fire bursts into life and I decide the time has come to haul the little stove out of the inferno and rescue both myself and the bothy from instant oblivion. Seeing me do this the spy, outside, comes in from the cold.

Charlie is pale and sweating. "Was that wise? I mean, was that a good idea?"

I sit in silence, watching the flames lick up the chimney, pondering Charlie's question. The phrases 'good idea' and 'wise' are usually co-dependent. If something is not a good idea, it can't be wise. In this case, however, as the warmth reaches my toes, I decide that my gas stove trick was definitely a good idea and absolutely, completely unwise. That's a bit like the paradox of bothies themselves: we go into the wild outdoors so we can be completely comfortable.

I can't emphasise enough that shoving your stove into a fire is not a good idea – just because I'd do it doesn't mean you should. That's cleared that up then.

* * *

Here's another, less dangerous tip I've learnt about lighting bothy fires. Take this common scenario:

You arrive at the bothy. It's dark, freezing and you are wet through. You throw your coal, kindling, and firelighters onto the fire, put a match to it and what happens?

As the fire begins to light it gives off a lot of smoke. The smoke rises, and as it does so it hits a column of cold air that's been sitting in the chimney since that bloke Burns was here three months ago and set fire to his trousers. The smoke cools, comes back down the chimney and fills the bothy. Unless you are a trainee kipper, this is very unpleasant, and it can take at least an hour before the chimney is finally warm enough for the smoke to behave itself and head out and up instead of into your sleeping bag. My trick is to put my gas stove in the fireplace – this time *before* you put any fuel in – and burn it for a few minutes. This will help move the cold air out of the chimney and may stop it smoking. It doesn't always work but it's worth a try.

Of course, if the fire won't light you now know what *not* to do.

Of Bothies And Bikes

As the hill steepens my legs ache with increasing vehemence. I keep pushing the pedals in the hope that the bike will suddenly find its way to the top of the hill. Glancing up, I can see the top of the road where the angle eases, but it looks a long way off. I reach for the gear lever to choose a lower gear only to find that there isn't one. My lungs are bursting and I can feel my heart trying to leap out of my chest. I give up the battle, stop the bike, and slump forward over the handlebars, my lungs dragging in air as if I've just surfaced from the depths of the ocean.

It is at this moment, when I am defeated and exhausted, that a Lycra-clad youth on a gleaming bike hurtles past me up the hill. His buttocks stand out of the saddle like two plums in a yellow hanky. His legs are made of iron and his calves bulge with muscle. He climbs the hill with the ease and grace of a gazelle dancing across the African plains. I climb the hill with the grace of hippo falling off a shed roof.

I am old, overweight, bald, exhausted and foolish; which is not a bad set for just a few minutes on a bike. I am all those things, but I am also determined. I climb back on the bike and begin to puff up the hill again. The incline is so steep it's hard to get moving, and just as I manage to wobble the bike into some forward motion, the young cyclist who passed me with such disdain meets me once more flying back down the hill. He is going so quickly I only catch a glimpse. His figure-hugging cycling suit matches his helmet and he looks simultaneously elegant and sinister in wraparound mirrored sunglasses.

In a split second he passes me and is gone, back towards Inverness, where I left home an eternity ago for a quick cycle up the hill. My legs hurt, and my backside feels as though the saddle is a knife edge. Slowly, painfully, I make progress until at last I am only a few yards from the summit. Then it happens again: the young man in Lycra passes me. He is doing repetitions of a hill I can barely get up.

"Hello," he calls to me cheerfully.

I look up, through the veil of sweat and pain, but I can't reply: I don't have enough breath.

His yellow backside disappears into the distance like a demented wasp and I wish he would suffer some catastrophic crash, my hatred for him is so intense.

That was taking up cycling, some time ago now. I eventually made it to the top of that hill; it gradually got less painful and a whole world of cycling opened up to me. My home town of Inverness has some of the best cycling routes anywhere. The hills south of Loch Ness offer a fantastic variety of routes into quiet countryside with lochs and hills aplenty.

If, on a summer's evening, you head out of town along the south side of Loch Ness you can ride some nine miles to the sleepy village of Dores with its little inn and tourists feeding grateful ducks. The route meanders through woods and fields, and even for a decrepit cyclist such as myself it's an easy, pleasant ride. If you want to linger there you can talk to the resident Nessie hunter who lives by the inn in a broken-down van and makes a living selling crude models of the creature he makes from beach pebbles. In over twenty years of scanning the waves with his binoculars, I don't think he has even caught so much as a glimpse of the beast. That he is still there is a triumph of optimism over reason.

From Dores you can cycle on, along the lochside, and pass by the house of the notorious occultist Aleister Crowley at Boleskine with its eerie graveyard. If you are more energetic you can turn left, away from the village, and enjoy a lung-bursting climb up into the hills with magnificent views across the loch to Drumnadrochit with its spectacular ruined castle.

Cycling out to the little village became my regular summer-evening pastime. After a day tied to my desk, it was wonderful to be able to hop on my bike and, in less than fifteen minutes, be out in the countryside smelling the scent of pine trees and listening to the buzz of insects. The encouraging thing about cycling is that you improve in a relatively short time. I quickly noticed that hills that had defeated me when I started ceased to be troublesome, and I climbed them in higher and higher gears. After I became moderately fit would go further afield, exploring the rolling foothills of the Monadhliath and allowing myself to become hypnotised by the rhythmic whirr of my tyres on the road.

I spread the map out on my dining room table and allowed my finger to follow the long winding track that leads from Poolewe to the remote bothy of Carnmore, a place I have never visited. One of the joys of exploring the Highlands – especially its remote bothies – is planning expeditions. I imagine what the views will be like and how it will feel to stand in that bothy door and enjoy the scenery of an evening. It occurs to me that Carnmore would be an obvious place to visit by bike, the only problem being that I own only a road bike and there is no way my flimsy creature would cope with the rigours of cycling, fully laden, in to a bothy.

Two weeks later I am the owner of the best mountain bike that I can buy – which is also the cheapest, as I don't have much money since I took early retirement. Full of enthusiasm I set out to Poolewe to begin my new plan of cycling in to as many bothies as possible. I load up my shiny new bike and head off down the track. At first the little path is fine, and I happily cycle along; but soon it narrows so much I have to get off and push. Then it narrows even more and I am forced to pick up the bike and carry it. I can't help thinking that I am doing something wrong here – is the bike not supposed to be carrying me?

A middle-aged woman walking her dogs appears around a bend in the track. She looks at me as if I am a lunatic. "I don't think this path is suitable for bikes. There's a much better track over there, you know." She points to the far side of the small lochan.

I smile benignly. I'm not about to give up. Further along the track it gets worse, and the bike starts to fight back. The wheels get snagged in every bush I pass and the pedals take lumps out of my shins and tear my trousers. Meanwhile the bike, using some process unknown to physics, gains mass and grows heavier by the minute. It's like being in one of those military tattoos where groups of large men have to manhandle a field gun across an imaginary gorge.

Eventually, sweating, swearing and bleeding, I emerge from the jungle to meet the wide, bike-friendly track I should have been on all the time. At the path junction there is a kennel where half a dozen Jack Russells take turns in barking at me through the bars. When I climb on the bike they fall silent, watching my departure.

"I'll show them. This is what I came for, the freedom of the open road."

I push off on the bike. Instantly I select the wrong gear, and the bike teeters wildly before hurling me to the ground as if it were an irate horse. For a moment I watch the sky roll past my feet before landing with a crunch in the gravel. The Jack Russells clearly haven't seen anything so funny for years, and burst out in hysterical laughter all barking at once. I pick myself up and glare at them. This only increases their enjoyment of the situation. My dignity in tatters – just like my trousers – I decide to give up and return home. Carnmore can wait another day, at least until I learn how to ride a mountain bike that is.

A week later, trousers repaired and legs healed, I set off to cycle to a bothy in the heart of the Monadhliath mountains. The Monadhliath covers a large area of rolling high country to the south of Inverness, running down to the Spey valley, as far as the villages of Kingussie and Newtonmore. Years ago, a naturalist friend told me in reverential whispers about this wild and untravelled land where wildlife flourished in abundance. I was fascinated by his description of the place and longed to visit it. Now, sadly, the Monadhliath are the best example of all that we do wrong to our hills. They are littered with wind farms and their flanks and summits are criss-crossed by mile after mile of bulldozed Land Rover tracks, leaving great scars across the landscape. If it were only the wind farms – which one could argue are a necessary evil to reduce our dependence upon fossil fuels – the Monadhliath would be relatively untouched as a wildlife area, but they are cursed by a greater evil: driven grouse shooting.

If you are unfamiliar with this practice it is a form of hunting where folk known as 'beaters' sweep across a hillside driving red grouse towards a line of men with shotguns. The shooters pay well for the privilege of killing the birds, and driven grouse shooting is a major source of income for the sporting estates that occupy the Monadhliath. It's not the shoots themselves that cause problems for the wildlife as much as how the land is managed. Grouse and other game birds are intensively managed on these moors and their numbers artificially boosted by feeding them disease-controlling medication. The habitat is also managed by burning the heather so that new shoots grow, which the grouse can feed on.

On many grouse moors, there are strenuous attempts to eradicate predators or anything that competes with the grouse for food. This includes the widespread slaughter of foxes, stoats and weasels, mountain hares (which is legal), and the trapping and poisoning of birds of prey such as eagles and hen harriers (which is not). The problem for the estates is that their customers want to shoot birds – so the more there are, the more satisfied their customers will be. By artificially increasing the numbers of red grouse, they create a magnet for predators of all kinds. Although legislation exists to protect birds of prey, many of the shooting estates are in remote areas and there are only a handful of wildlife crime police officers covering the whole of Scotland.

Prosecutions for the illegal killing of wildlife are rare even though many bodies, such as the RSPB and National Park Authorities, believe the practice to be widespread. The Scottish parliament is currently considering legislation requiring driven grouse moors to be licensed, which may be the beginning of some degree of control. Until now, sporting estates – which occupy huge chunks of the Highlands – have been able to do pretty much what they like. Walk across a driven grouse moor and you are walking through a denuded wildlife desert, managed exclusively for the profit of a tiny percentage of the population.

The bothy I am trying to cycle to is locked and has been for years. That's a shame as it lies right at the centre of the Monadhliath. If it were open it would mean that you could walk, using bothies for overnight stays, right across this area. I climb on my bike, hoping to get where I'm going this time. To my left the river Findhorn swirls and boils in beautiful pools where trout rise, and I catch sight of a kingfisher, a flash of shining green and blue. On either side of the river the hills rise a hundred different shades of brown and green on this summer's day. Despite the fact that the track is almost level I'm finding it hard going and have to drop down through the gears; I'm heading straight into a strong westerly wind and it's pushing me back almost as hard as I can pedal.

I make it a few miles up the glen, as far as Coignafearn Lodge, an impressive ancestral pile with a giant front door designed to repel all invaders. This is the 'big house' of the estate. I count twenty chimneys rising from the roof and imagine a poor maid running from one room to the other desperately trying to light every fireplace simultaneously while his lordship stamps about waiting impatiently for his morning porridge. In the end I have to surrender and admit the wind has defeated me. I turn the bike around and, with the wind behind, I'm back at my car in only a few minutes. I have failed again at mountain biking.

Despite my disastrous start at mountain biking I am beginning to learn a few things about the sport. The term 'mountain bike' is a misnomer. They should really be called 'track bikes', because that's what they are designed for. In order to ride one up a mountain you'd need nuclear-powered legs; in order to ride one down you'd have to either not care if you got to the bottom alive or have already written a suicide note. If you see a boulder in your way as you head down the hill, do something about it right away. What you do doesn't really matter – your life is already hanging in the balance and it's probably a matter of chance whether you survive or not – but if you spend any time at all trying to decide what to do, you will have already hit the boulder and parted company from the bike several seconds before you try and act.

Fortune favours the brave on a mountain bike. Nine times out of ten the best thing to do is go for it, as the bike is capable of doing things you didn't think possible. This means 10 per cent of the time going for it is not the best thing to do and you will end up chewing gravel. This is unfortunate, but almost 100 per cent of the time if you hesitate the deadly wobble factor will take over and you will *definitely* taste the aggregate.

Cycling up a steep hill is the nearest thing there is to

purgatory that you can experience without an invitation from the devil himself to visit his place of abode. You will discover you can sweat from places you didn't know you had and, at least in the Highlands of Scotland, if you can't pedal fast enough, the horde of biting insects close behind will catch up and devour you.

The hell of pedalling uphill is, however, more than compensated for by the blessed relief and exhilaration of hurtling back down the hill. On the way down, you will cover ground in milliseconds that took you hours to cover on the way up. The flies that tormented you in ascent will be blown away on the way down. You will experience untold but short-lived joy that will convince you (erroneously) that it was all worth it.

Mountain bikes have really good brakes. That might sound obvious but I didn't know this until I was cycling home from the pub and a taxi driver decided he wasn't going to bother looking for bikes and pulled out in front of me. I slammed on the brakes and the bike squealed to a halt. If I'd been on my road bike I would have collided with the side of the cab and enjoyed an aerial view of the taxi on the start of my journey to hospital.

This time I tell myself I am going to make it, even if it kills me, as (I was beginning to believe) it certainly will. The first eight miles or so are fine. I manage to ride the bike most of the way into Glen Beag to get to the little bothy deep in the Highland glen. All is good until the Land Rover track I am riding stops and runs into a bog.

They say you should try everything once. Let me save you the trouble of trying this experience, just take my word for it: pushing a heavily laden mountain bike through a peat bog is absolutely no fun at all. It's like trying to heave my grandmother, sitting on a settee eating chips, across the Himalayas. (She was big woman, my grandmother.) In fact if I had managed to enter purgatory without having had this experience I wouldn't have been too upset at all.

Glenbeg was the first bothy I ever visited. A group of us got permission to drive down the track and walk the last mile or so to the little shelter nestling in the shadow of Ben Dearg. I was amazed at the remoteness of the place and a whole world opened up for me. I had no idea such places existed and I have been exploring them ever since. A young guy called Martin, whom everyone called Tintin because of his remarkable resemblance to Hergé's boy hero, suggested we gather fire wood.

I was a bit confused when we stepped out of the bothy as I couldn't see a tree for miles. To my amazement Tintin started digging. Quickly he unearthed a sodden piece of tree root well on its way to becoming peat.

"There!" he announced gleefully. "Part of the old forest, that."

I had known that the Highlands were once covered in forest but until that moment I never realised that in many glens the remnants of primordial woodlands lie only inches below the surface of the peat. He had found part of a tree stump cut by the hand of a crofter hundreds of years ago. I looked dubiously at the gnarled old lump of wood.

"That'll never burn," I told him.

Twenty minutes later we were sitting before a roaring fire. I had discovered the joy of bogwood.

Today I despair of reaching the place and consider

abandoning the bike and walking the last half mile, carrying the panniers. But then, I decide, I wouldn't have got there by bike and a third failure is inconceivable. Last time I wrote of my failure some ardent mountain bikers, scornful of the ineptitude of a sixty-year-old man on his first mountain bike, informed me that I should get the weight out of my rucksack and on to the bike. I now own a shiny new set of panniers and biking has become a lot easier.

Inch by inch the bothy grows closer. As I step out of the bog and stand only a hundred yards from my home for the night, I realise I can hear a faint roar. I've heard that roar before and know that it can only mean one thing: a river. Perhaps, I hope, the river is at the far side of the bothy and I won't have to cross it. How foolishly hopeful the human spirit is, for I can see the river, fast, furious and between me and the bothy door. Rivers like that are *always* between you and the bothy. I've never seen one that was on the far side so you don't have to cross it to get there. What would be the fun in that?

I'm too tired to take off my boots and just plunge through the torrent bike and all. Moments later I push open the door of the little shelter and I'm there. Glenbeg is no longer maintained by the Mountain Bothies Association (MBA) and has slipped off the hillwalker's radar. The place looks a bit sorry for itself, and I wonder if I'm the first person there this year (it's early April as I write this). Somehow you can tell this place is rarely visited now. Thick dust lies everywhere and the air is musty; it feels as if the old bothy has become a lonely place. I feel sorry for the little shelter as, without some care and maintenance, it must surely fall to ruin.

Outside the bothy my red mountain bike sits, muddied but unbowed, and I feel proud that I have at last cycled in to my first bothy. I wonder how many more two-wheeled adventures lie ahead.

We Are Legends

It went dark a long, long time ago and we are still walking. My boots are full of water, the result of sinking into a bog, and I'm weighed down by my rucksack full of climbing gear. Looking back I see Charlie's head torch bobbing along behind me, heading for the same bog I just fell into. I should call out and warn him, but I am too tired to shout, and we have both fallen into so many bogs, in this interminable descent, that another won't make much difference. I plod on, lost in a world of aching legs and exhaustion, and wonder idly if Charlie will find the bog.

"Oh, for fuck's sake!" I hear him cry out in the darkness. He found the bog.

* * *

The lure of Scottish winters drew me north. It was June when I arrived in the Highland capital of Inverness and moved in to a small, run-down flat in a row of old fisherman's cottages beside the River Ness. The kitchen was damp and mouse infested, and the few items of furniture were threadbare. I didn't care. It suited me. From my doorstep I could see distant mountains and a river that was so clean I could watch seals hunting for salmon. For the boy who grew up beside the River Mersey, thick with oil and chemicals, this was a glimpse of paradise. I spent the summer exploring the hills and climbing on some lowland crags. That was fun enough but, through those early months, I was waiting for snow to arrive and for the great game to start.

I was in the mountaineering club one night when a young man with a twisted and scarred face came and sat down beside me.

"They tell me you're a climber?"

He was clearly several pints into the evening's entertainment and swayed a little on the chair.

"Well, I've done a bit."

He looked at me as though studying some complex puzzle. "Do you climb in winter?"

I opened my mouth to respond but he didn't wait for an answer.

"Can you handle exposure?" he said pointedly.

I wasn't too sure if I could or not. "Well, I've climbed in the Alps." That seemed to satisfy him.

He was known as 'Glasgow Charlie' by the mountaineering club regulars who told me, in whispered tones, of him leaping off cliffs into icy gullies and climbing wild routes no one else would attempt. Charlie did not work, being temperamentally unsuited to employment. A few years earlier he had deserted from the Rhodesian army and lived with his long-suffering mother who more or less supported him. His life mainly consisted of drinking, pursuing women, and climbing – pretty much in that order. The only problem he had was outwitting the Job Centre who seemed to have some odd notion that he should work for his living. He had a wicked sense of humour, and we slowly became friends, so it seemed natural we should climb together.

* * *

Charlie stands at the foot of the icy cliff and stares upwards studying the face. He points to a prow of rock that stands out from the crag. "See, there it is. You go up that sort of crack onto that block and then step round the corner onto the face and you're basically up. That's the climb over."

I look at the prow of rock, trying to follow the line he can see, but no matter how hard I search I can't see a route up.

Charlie lights up an acrid hand-rolled cigarette and casually scratches his chin. "It'll be a piece of cake."

I look at the rock face again, but I can't see any cake.

* * *

We are in the Northern Corries of the Cairngorms on a cold January day under a milky grey sky. The day is still, and a thin mist veils the crags. On this windless day the calls of other climbing parties echo eerily around the corrie. Charlie and I have been climbing together now for almost two years and a bond of experience and trust has grown between us as our skills in the mountains have grown. Despite this trust I still can't manage to see the climbing route – what climbers call a 'line' – that Charlie has made out.

Charlie sets off up the cliff, climbing in a relaxed unorthodox fashion that only he can pull off. Charlie does nothing by the rules, either in the mountains or in the rest of his life; he is a wild free spirit and the only law he obeys is gravity.

He sets up the first belay. "There you are. No bother. I can't think why no one's climbed this route before."

I take the lead for the next pitch. As I climb, the route begins to steepen. After an awkward corner I find myself standing on the block Charlie pointed out from the corrie floor.

He calls up to me excitedly. "Just step round the corner and onto the face and you'll be up."

I study the rock. The face looks holdless and vertical with a tiny ripple I can step onto but nothing for my hands. I try to make the move, but with each attempt I feel myself pitching backwards and have to retreat. A long, serious fall looks inevitable if I leave the security of the block.

Charlie shouts encouragement. "Just step onto the face."

"You step onto the bloody face, I'm coming down."

He tries but, like me, can't make the move. We abseil off and find that a small group has been watching our spectacular failure from the base of the cliff.

An enthusiastic red-faced youth waves a guidebook at me. "I can't see a climb up there in the book. Prospecting new routes? Well done."

"Prospecting new falls more like," I reply, and Charlie laughs.

On the drive back to Inverness I mimic the sound of a hospital heart monitor. "Beep, beep, beep. Step onto the face, Charlie says. I walked two paces yesterday and tomorrow the doctor says I might be able to have a spoonful of vegetable soup if they can squeeze it though the hole in my full-body plaster cast. Step onto the face my arse. Are you trying to bloody kill me?"

Charlie roars with laughter, belching acrid smoke as he does so. He and I climbed together for several years after that until I moved away to live on the Isle of Skye and our climbing partnership came to an end.

* * *

Ten years later I call him on the phone and, after some persuasion, he agrees to climb with me again. It's December and the Highland days are desperately short. Early snow brings the mountains alive and, as we walk in to the climb, the morning sun touches the summits and turns them crimson. The North-East Ridge of Aonach Beag is a hidden gem of a route, tucked away in a distant corrie. Our plan was to catch the cable car to the ski runs on a nearby mountain, thereby saving us a very long walk in, but they were closed for maintenance so there is no alternative but to make the long walk around Ben Nevis.

It's a beautiful December morning, cold, crisp and bright. As we walk up the long glen I feel sorry for the poor souls still lying in bed and missing this natural glory. After a few hours our goal comes into sight: an elegant ridge sweeping up from the valley floor to the summit far above us. Soon we are weaving our way upwards between short cliffs, until the ridge steepens and narrows to a crest and the climb proper begins. Charlie leads up a steep icy corner and I can see that his ability on rock and ice has not been diminished.

Around the corner, I am leading when I encounter a wide snowslope. From the valley floor it had looked crisp, white and enticing, the kind of snow winter climbers dream of. This, however, is not that kind of snow. This snow is fresh, soft, and worst of all sticky. The Eskimos have fifty words for different kinds of snow and I have one for this type: crap.

As I try to climb the spikes of my crampons became entombed in football-sized snowballs and the whole slope threatens to part company from the mountain and drag me down with it into the jaws of the valley waiting, open mouthed, below.

By now the shadows are becoming ominously long and our progress worryingly slow. It's crunch time – do we carry on and risk being caught on the climb in darkness or do we retreat now and face the long walk back? If we can get to the summit the way home will be a lot quicker.

"Charlie," I call. "We'd better go down. If we carry on we'll end up on here in the dark."

I am, of course, wrong – it's already too late. The darkness overtakes us on the descent and a nightmare ensues as we weave between cliffs whose height we cannot judge in the dark. Eventually we are confronted by a cliff we cannot circumvent.

We are unroped as Charlie peers over the cliff into the darkness below. "Och, it's not far. I think I can jump this."

In my head, on the control panel that monitors what is happening, all the warning lights turn red. I visualise Charlie falling over the cliff like a drunk slipping silently off a kerb.

"Come back – for god's sake don't jump."

He hesitates on the brink of oblivion, exhausted, his brain fogged, so I yell at him again and this time he turns and joins me where we rope up. I look around for a belay but can find nothing.

"I'll lower you off," I tell him, knowing I can rely on my strength to take is weight.

He looks at me dubiously. "How will you get down?"

"I don't know."

In crisis I break things down into simple steps. I want to get him down the cliff safely, then I'll worry about the next problem, me. I lower him slowly over the edge and watch his head torch vanish into the darkness. After a few moments there's a cry and the rope goes slack; he's down!

Now I must look for an anchor point to abseil off the cliff. I scour the rock face and notice a tiny blade of grass growing out of the rock I had not noticed before. If there is grass there must be soil; if there is soil there must be a crack; if there is a crack it might take a rock peg that I can lower myself from. The crack is small, and the peg only goes in halfway, but perhaps it will hold me.

I lower myself very slowly over the cliff edge, trying to put as little weight on the peg as possible. I can see Charlie about seventy feet below me. The abseil takes an eternity and at every moment I expect the anchor to fail and to plummet to earth. At last my feet touch down on the bed of the gully. Wordlessly, Charlie passes me a cigarette.

Surrounded by the immense darkness, we begin our walk back to the road. At last, our legs rubbery with exhaustion from descending through the endless bog, we hit the path through Glen Nevis.

Charlie collapses. "Leave me here to die. Seriously, it would be a kindness."

I hurl a chocolate biscuit at him in the hope the sugar will revive him. We both roll cigarettes and spend a few minutes sucking in the delicious, acrid smoke.

"This will pass into legend. It'll become a myth." We both chuckle.

We head off down the glen, despairing of our failure, like two one-time badass gunfighters who have been run out of town by the Milky Bar Kid.

These were the days before the internet when friends were people you had actually met. If you wanted to know about climbs and climbers, you had to meet members of the outdoors brotherhood in the corners of drinking dens. At first, they'd tell you very little until, by some mysterious process, you had displayed sufficient courage to be accepted into the fraternity. Then they would whisper tales of the great feats of other climbers – heroes who had faced the monsters of the mountains head on. Sometimes these tales would be of conquests but more often of heroic failure, for disaster always makes a better story.

Over the telling the tales would grow; falls would become longer, climbs more desperate and their combatants bolder and more foolish in equal measure. So too would the tale of our long walk, through the deep blackness of this mountain night, be told. We would tell it over beers in the pub in some distant future place; we would laugh at our ineptitude, relive our terror, until the story had become absorbed into the folklore of our brotherhood.

The next few miles pass by in a fog of exhaustion. I find the river and follow the path as it turns right. Charlie doesn't see the path turn and wanders into the river, but we are both so wet it doesn't matter. Around midnight two old climbers plod into the car park and climb into their waiting car, seventeen hours after leaving it.

* * *

A few years later Charlie and I are sitting drinking quietly in the bar at the mountaineering club's weekly meet. On the other side of the room a group of young climbers are talking and laughing loudly.

One of them quietens the others and turns to me with a grin. "Hey John. How long was it you two were on the North-East Ridge of Aonach Beag, twenty-one hours wasn't it?"

"Oh, I think it was longer than that," Charlie says, his eyes twinkling.

There is a roar of laughter from the other table.

We are legends.

Gelder Shiel Bothy

Thirty years have passed since I walked up past the entrance to Balmoral Castle and into the forest beyond. As I head up the forestry track I pass the neat, well-maintained cottages that are home to the estate workers. As this is the Queen's Highland residence, I half expect to be confronted by guardsmen and I wonder if, somewhere in the castle, a security guard is watching an old man, weighed down by a rucksack, plodding slowly past the ornate wrought-iron gates. The forested section is steeper than I remember it. I'm breathing heavily under my load of coal, sleeping bag, food and whisky by the time I emerge from the forest and out onto the open hillside.

The glen is broad and open, the outlines of the snow-covered hills etched white against the darkening skies. The silhouette of the mountain, Lochnagar, looms above the glen as a herd of deer trickles over the shoulder of the hills. Out of the shelter of the forest the wind is cold against my cheek and, as the light begins to fade and the evening turns to night, I am suddenly conscious of how empty this place is. The wide valley is treeless apart from one small cluster of trees a couple of miles away. It is to that stand of trees I am heading, for hidden there is Gelder Shiel bothy, my home for the night.

Charlie and I had aimed for that same group of trees one

winter's night thirty years ago. It had been dark then and a pale moon had picked out the trees, black against a sea of thigh-deep snow. That night we had lingered in the pub and thought the walk in to the remote bothy would be little more than a stroll, but we had not realised that a recent blizzard had carpeted the landscape above the tree line with deep snow. Charlie swayed across the hill. In the deep snow neither of us had any idea if we were on the path or not. I had watched Charlie, with his wild hair and rolling gait, track back and forth across the snow before finally having to admit that the path was lost.

Back then our rucksacks were crammed with rope, crampons and ice axes, as we planned to do battle with the ice-clad cliffs of Lochnagar. The mountain had an air of foreboding. It seemed wild and remote, its winter climbs legendary for their ferocity. It was after midnight before the pair of us staggered through the bothy doorway. Thirty years ago Gelder Shiel was a grim place on a bitterly cold winter's night. There was no fireplace and the bare whitewashed walls gave little protection from the icy night air. Exhausted, we climbed in to our sleeping bags and slept fitfully on the hard wood of the bunk beds, shivering now and again as the cold gripped the place.

Today, as I push open the door of the bothy, knowing that the Mountain Bothies Association have done a great deal of work here, I am hoping for a more comfortable night. I look around in amazement. Gone are the bleak frozen walls I remember; no longer do the stones drip with condensation. Now the little one-room bothy is insulated and lined with wood and, joy of joys, in the corner stands a wood-burning stove, a serious fire capable of warming the bones of any old man foolish enough to wander this way. There is even a small supply of wood, provided by the Queen's estate, and since I have carried in coal, a warm night is guaranteed.

Thirty years ago, Charlie and I awoke to an arctic landscape. During the night another snowstorm had swept in, contributing a few more inches to the already deep snow. High on Lochnagar itself the storm still raged and we climbed up into the corrie almost blinded, feeling our way to the base of the cliffs. This was my first winter climbing season and the prospect of meeting the great beast of Lochnagar filled me with a heady mixture of dread and excitement. Soon, through the swirling snow, a vague outline of the great cliff loomed above us still largely shrouded in the white clouds of falling flakes. We headed upwards and found ourselves in a broad gully that, though choked with snow, offered little resistance. Charlie and I climbed upwards through the soft snow with great towers of rock emerging on either side as we approached the summit of the mountain.

Emboldened by our success, we followed the guidebook and found a harder route to follow. I had a brand-new piece of kit I was desperate to try out, a snow anchor known as a Deadman. This was a thin metal plate about the size of a large book that, placed at the correct angle, would slice into the snow and hold any fall. I placed the Deadman in the snow and pulled on it. To my amazement it dutifully buried itself deeper and I was convinced that it would hold us if we fell.

Soon we were on alarmingly steep ice and my fledgling skills were being severely tested. I drove my axes into the ice and stepped up onto the front spikes of my crampons. This technique, known as front pointing, was what I had been seeking to employ since I began winter climbing. Now that I was doing it for real it felt precarious in the extreme and I wasn't too sure I wanted to do it again. Charlie and I climbed higher, up soft unstable snow and out onto the face where the ice steepened. Here we were exposed to the full ferocity of the wind and were batterd by blown snow. Following Charlie up and over the final few feet of the cliff, my hands became frozen, immobile with the cold. I held my ice axes in two frozen claws as I at last pulled over onto the ice-blasted summit of the mountain.

Those moments, decades ago, came back to me in vivid technicolour as I sat in the newly refurbished bothy and watched the cherry-red flames take hold of the coal in the stove. I remembered how elated we had been as we walked back to the bothy. We had completed our first real winter climb, a rite of passage. We had fought the demon and won. That climb began an obsession that was to rule my life for the next ten years.

Sitting with my whisky before the glowing fire I realise now that we had been unknowingly dicing with death that winter's day long ago. After the recent snowfall, the face was dangerously avalanche prone but we had climbed on, full of the bravado and ignorance of youth. Only luck saved us from catastrophe; enthusiasm and inexperience are a dangerous mix in this game of ice and iron. Most climbing accidents do not happen to those tackling the hardest routes. They happen to novices, straying for the first time onto easy gullies, trying to develop their winter skills.

Thirty years on I hurl another log onto the fire and remember the cold of thirty years ago. Charlie and I had been lucky – we had tempted the mountain gods but they had chosen to treat us kindly and hold back the avalanches hanging above our heads. I no longer feel the need to test myself in the arena of winter climbing but I am glad that I can still come to these wild places and sit with contentment before the open fire.

Curious to see the night sky, I push open the door. The frosty air hits me and reminds me of the cold all those years ago. Above, a carpet of stars shines down from the eternal sky.

A few yards from the bothy is a small cottage reputedly used for afternoon tea by the Queen's shooting parties. I've no doubt that Queen Victoria, accompanied by Mr Brown, her favourite ghillie, used to pause here on their rides through the royal estate. High in the clear night sky the stars twinkle and I watch as two young men, the ghosts of my youth, head towards the mountain, ice axes jingling, sharing a joke in the early morning.

Lachin y Gair

Away, ye gay landscapes, ye gardens of roses!
In you let the minions of luxury rove;
Restore me the rocks where the snowflake reposes,
Though still they are sacred to freedom and love:
Yet, Caledonia, belov'd are thy mountains,
Round their white summits though elements war;
Though cataracts foam, 'stead of smooth-flowing fountains,
I sigh for the valley of dark Loch na Garr.
Ah! there my young footsteps in infancy, wander'd:
My cap was the bonnet, my cloak was the plaid;
On chieftains, long perish'd, my memory ponder'd,
As daily I strode through the pine-cover'd glade;

I sought not my home, till the day's dying glory
Gave place to the rays of the bright polar star;
For fancy was cheer'd, by traditional story,
Disclos'd by the natives of dark Loch na Garr.

"Shades of the dead! have I not heard your voices
Rise on the night-rolling breath of the gale?"
Surely, the soul of the hero rejoices,
And rides on the wind, o'er his own Highland vale!
Round Loch na Garr, while the stormy mist gathers,
Winter presides in his cold icy car:
Clouds, there, encircle the forms of my Fathers;
They dwell in the tempests of dark Loch na Garr.

"Ill starr'd, though brave, did no visions foreboding
Tell you that fate had forsaken your cause?"
Ah! were you destined to die at Culloden,
Victory crown'd not your fall with applause:
Still were you happy, in death's earthy slumber,
You rest with your clan, in the caves of Braemar;
The Pibroch[6] resounds, to the piper's loud number,
Your deeds, on the echoes of dark Loch na Garr.

Years have roll'd on, Loch na Garr, since I left you,
Years must elapse, ere I tread you again:
Nature of verdure and flowers has bereft you,
Yet still are you dearer than Albion's plain:
England! thy beauties are tame and domestic,
To one who has rov'd on the mountains afar:

Oh! for the crags that are wild and majestic,
The steep, frowning glories of dark Loch na Garr
—George Gordon Byron

Gasherbrum, Masherbrum, Distaghil Sar,
they're jolly good training for dark Lochnagar.
—Tom Patey

Ben Alder Cottage

My head-torch beam picks out the lettering on the faded rail timetable, and my breath mists in the cold air as I try to read the tiny digits. There is a train in two hours according to the timetable pinned to the wall in the tiny station shelter but, on this dark winter's night, I am finding it hard to believe. I read the sign again to be sure I am not mistaken, but no – if timetables are to be believed at all, this one is adamant that a train is coming.

It is March and I am on the platform of the highest railway station in Britain, Corrour. That there is a station in this vast empty space at all is incongruous. I had arrived just as the light was beginning to die and had watched as the mountains around me faded into silhouettes and then, as the darkness became deeper still, even their massive outlines were swallowed by the blackness.

I thrust my hands deep into the pockets of my duvet jacket, grateful for the warmth it brings, and plod along the station platform (there is only one). The frost-encrusted platform sparkles in the light of my torch as the temperature keeps dropping. Around me there is only impenetrable blackness, undisturbed by even a pinprick of light. I am trapped here now, utterly dependent on the arrival of the promised train to take me back to my car parked outside the station at Spean Bridge.

I'm frustrated by the notion that I shouldn't be here at all; I should be sitting beside the fire in Ben Alder Cottage bothy, gently dozing. I am pondering the injustice of it all when there is an explosion of light somewhere out in the darkness. The silence is rent apart as a train – the Caledonian Sleeper, heading for London, the opposite direction to my journey – comes screeching to a halt.

I can hear the engine throbbing and see humanity peering back at me through the carriage windows. The passengers look at me curiously, alien travellers from the world of cars and machines; they are creatures of light and warmth while I exist in a world of darkness and ice. The guard opens a door and peers at me for a few seconds before closing it again and vanishing. The train sits, lights glaring, throbbing and hissing like a great dragon. Anxious eyes peer at me from the confines of the carriages as if they are wondering why anyone would be 'out there'. I am a creature of the wild.

"Are you getting on?" the guard asks after peering from his carriage door for the third time. They seem reluctant to leave me here, perhaps concerned about my fate in the wilderness.

"I'm going the other way. North," I explain.

The guard looks at me, bewildered, and slams the door. As the train pulls away, I see pity in the eyes of its passengers. They obviously think I have been left to freeze to death on the platform, perhaps a result of not having the correct fare. With alarming speed, the train recedes into the distance and once more I am in a silent dark world with only my thoughts for company.

Eight hours earlier I had stepped onto that same platform and into a very different world. The sky had been a cloudless blue and, even in the early morning, its rays had carried some heat. I had been sweating gently as I set off along the long track that runs beside Loch Ossian and into the hills beyond. That morning the loch had stretched way into the distance, its surface mirror smooth on that windless day. Above the loch the mountain ridges, still topped with snow, shone in the morning sun so brightly it hurt to look at them too long. I was headed for Ben Alder Cottage, the legendary bothy beside Loch Ericht, and had many miles to walk.

Following the path beside Loch Ossian had been easy and, even though this was only March, it felt as though spring had arrived early as I crossed the bridge at the head of the loch. The birds sang and the sun shone as I passed by the small estate buildings that service Corrour estate. I could only glimpse Corrour Lodge through the trees but, from what I could see, it is a unique building, with high curved walls split by a huge shard of glass windows. This is an odd place to erect something as architecturally dramatic. There are a great many big houses hidden away in remote glens across the Highlands – many are the playgrounds of the wealthy, and some are even bought by people just so they can say they own an estate in Scotland. I'm not envious of such people. As long as I am able to visit these place, impecunious as I am, the rich are welcome to their playthings.

The path dwindled as I climbed away from the lodge and up into the higher reaches of the glen where the hills began to crowd in around me. High on the mountain I watched a herd of deer sweep down from the higher tops and across the high pass that leads down to Loch Ericht and Ben Alder Cottage. I could only watch in awe as their sleek brown bodies glided across the terrain, covering in only a few minutes ground it would take me over an hour to cover.

Between me and the pass I needed to cross to get to the bothy there was a small river – or at least what should have been a small river. It's then I realised that the unseasonably warm conditions were melting the high snows and filling the burns and rivers with meltwater. The gentle river I needed to cross was now a cauldron of white foaming water and quite impossible. Reluctantly I deposited the little sack of coal I was carrying behind a boulder and set off on the long walk back to Corrour station. Night began to fall as I stepped on to the platform.

I watch as the Caledonian Sleeper train departs into the blackness. Two hours later there is another explosion of light and a little tube of civilisation screeches to a stop in front of me. I bound for the door and, seconds later, I am in a world of heat and light as the train speeds away into the darkness. I find the guard and ask her for tea. She begins to explain that, as the train will shortly reach its destination, she has closed the kitchen. Then she looks at me and catches the desperation in my eyes. Stepping off that frozen platform I may as well have stepped on to a spaceship headed for Mars. The other passengers are shoppers on their way home from Glasgow, families playing cards and businessmen dozing after meetings. All of them look at me incredulously. I am dressed for Siberia, I am the walker who came in from the cold.

* * *

Fast forward to October. I climb off the train and on to Corrour station once more. This is the place where they filmed the scene from *Trainspotting*, and it has become a Mecca for film buffs who step off the train and shiver for a few minutes before returning to the known world. The day is typical of an October day in the Highlands. Clouds race across the sky, and the surface of the loch, which had been glassy calm in March, is crossed by white horses in the fresh autumnal wind. I retrace my steps past the loch and past the grand lodge with its surreal architecture on up the glen to where I dumped my coal in the winter. The coal is there, undisturbed for all these months. I load it into my sack and head for the pass.

This time the river is no barrier: the wild, churning waters of March are reduced to a gentle trickle that laps at the soles of my boots like a friendly puppy. The climb up to the pass is less friendly. So far, I have been walking on Land Rover tracks or good paths but the section from the floor of the valley is trackless and steep. By the time I reach the top of the pass, I am sweating and puffing, acutely aware of the bag of coal in my rucksack. Walking through broken trackless ground is always exhausting and any track, no matter how vague, makes backpacking so much easier.

As I descend towards Loch Ericht the expanse of water unfurls below me like a great sheet of hammered grey gunmetal and, at last, six months after I first set off, the tiny black cottage comes into view. Loch Ericht is a long, deep loch that pierces through the hills like a knife slash. By the time I push open the door, curtains of rain are sweeping down the loch and I am grateful for the shelter of this humble dwelling.

Ben Alder cottage is a long, low building. Inside, the familiar smell of woodsmoke greets me along with a hint of old socks. Once, every human house smelled like this. I go into my familiar routine: I eat my steak and potatoes, light the fire and relax, revelling in my minor victory of having finally made it to the bothy. As darkness falls I am rewarded by the sight of rain falling steadily onto the surface of the loch whilst I drink my tea, warm and dry beside the fire. Such simple pleasures are the reward of the bothy hunter.

There are several sparsely furnished rooms in the cottage and one with a decent hearth. Ben Alder Cottage is well known for its supposed ghost. I think practically every bothy I have slept in claims some supernatural presence. My view is that most hauntings are down to the overactive imaginations of the occupants, flickering candlelight and a surfeit of whisky. Though I've spent many nights in bothies, I've never been troubled by a ghostly encounter. But in Ben Alder Cottage I did wonder if this might change – there are so many accounts of pots and pans being thrown about in the middle of the night and other unexplained occurrences.

One account suggests that the ghost in Ben Alder Cottage is a ghillie who hung himself from the rafters. Another gruesome explanation is that it is the ghost of a woman who was trapped in the bothy by a snowstorm and forced to eat her own child. I'm glad to say that the night I spent in the bothy was undisturbed by visitors from the other side, or any other place for that matter. I suspect that the ghost stories were invented to deter some folk from visiting the place. In the 1800s the bothy was renowned as a place where navvies and tramps would spend the night as they traversed the mountains. I think the owners wanted to dissuade folk as disreputable as me from staying there.

Ben Alder Cottage is also made famous by being featured in the novel *Kidnapped* by Robert Louis Stevenson. In the novel, the two heroes David Balfour and Alan Stewart are sheltered in the cottage by the clan chief Cluny MacPherson. This part of the story is based on truth – MacPherson actually existed and did hide on the slopes of the mountain when being hunted by British troops after the Jacobite defeat in 1745. He managed to hold out in the mountains for nine years before escaping to France and must have visited the bothy many times during that period. That anyone could hide themselves for that long testifies to just how remote the area must have been at a time when many of the empty glens we see today were populated. In the mid-18th century the Clearances were yet to take full effect.

After an undisturbed night I woke to find the rainclouds of the previous evening had dispersed and only a stiff breeze troubled the surface of the loch. My plan was not to return to Courour station, but to walk south, around the eastern shore of Loch Ericht, and make my way to Rannoch station and return to my car at Spean Bridge by that route. At first the track down the lochside was sketchy – surprising for what must be the most direct route in to the bothy. Soon I was picking my way through the trees until I came to a modern shooting cabin at the end of the loch. I tried the door – sorry, force of habit – and found it locked, then made my way across the remaining mile of ground towards the dam at the loch's end. That proved much harder than it sounds as the terrain was the composition of green blancmange and I had to pick my way through a never-ending quagmire of sphagnum moss.

Years ago I was involved in a mountain rescue nearby. It involved a youth group from the Birmingham area and was the only rescue I was ever involved in that was caused by such negligence I would consider it criminal. We were called out to a group of youngsters, aged between 11 and 18, who had set off to walk in to Ben Alder Cottage. The plan was that they would spend the night there and then walk out, but they had not appeared at the arranged rendezvous. By the time we crammed ourselves into a boat and set off for the southern shore of the loch these young people had already spent one night in the open and would soon be enduring their second, a potentially serious situation.

The southern shore of Loch Ericht has no path and is densely vegetated so moving any distance along it is difficult. Four of us landed while the rest of the team and a Sea King helicopter searched the area of the loch, which was by now in pitch darkness. When we hit the shore we split up; I headed west with another team member and two others went east. The eastern party were forced to wade out into the loch to make any progress due to the jumbled boulders and tangle of trees and bushes. They had not gone far when they heard cries for help. What they found shocked everyone in the team.

Eight children were huddled together on the shoreline. All were dressed in cotton tracksuits and trainers, ill equipped for a walk in the park, let alone crossing some of the remotest country in the UK. They had been 'led' by two 18-year-old girls who had no experience or training and had panicked and deserted the younger children. We found the older girls two hours later, hiding in a Land Rover. In all my time in mountain rescue I don't think I saw any situation where a group had been sent out into the hills so inadequately equipped or prepared. The weather on both nights was unusually mild; had it rained there could easily have been a tragedy.

Eventually I made it to the tarmac and decided I would hitch-hike to the station at Rannoch, fearful that if I walked the whole way I might miss the train and have to spend hours on the platform waiting for the next. Hitch-hiking seemed a good plan until I discovered there were absolutely no cars passing in the direction of the station. The road I was on, down the shore of Loch Rannoch, is a dead end so no one ever passes down there.

I set off walking, calculating that if I kept going at a reasonable pace I would just make the earlier train. After four miles, two miles from the station, a car slewed to a halt. Inside were a mother and her three children. They very kindly crammed my bulky body and even bulkier rucksack into the back seat and we all set off for the station with the youngest of the children happily telling me how they were going to see the station from Harry Potter. I was squashed in the back, unable to move, and the family's Labrador leant over from the boot of the car and spent the whole journey exploring my ears with his tongue.

The little station at Rannoch boasted a tea shop where a tired walker could indulge in tea and carrot cake and keep an eye open for wizards. Soon the train whisked me back to civilisation, leaving Ben Alder Cottage to its supernatural visitors.

A Night In Two-Hat Bothy

I'm an hour late arriving on the ridge that overlooks Bearnais bothy. An hour shouldn't matter much, but this hour does because this hour makes the difference between arriving in daylight and looking for the bothy by the glow of the moon. My pack weighs heavily on my back. It's full of wonderful things, like coal to keep me warm, tins of curry, baked beans and a chilli con carne I cooked myself. I've even got a tablet so I can watch a movie and some whisky that will warm me from the inside while the coal does its work from the other direction. I'll soon be glad of all these items I've carried for miles over the hills and through the snow, or at least I will be as long as I can do one thing: find the bothy.

The darkness brings a colder wind. Snow devils swirl about me and I am suddenly aware, staring down into the empty glen, of how alone I am. I fix a compass bearing and look along it to where the bothy should be, half a mile away. My eyes scan the snow and the ghostly outlines of stream beds for something angular, something man made that will give away the presence of the little shelter, but nothing appears. Perhaps, I think to myself, I should have bought a GPS after all – then all I'd need to do would be to switch it on and satellites above the earth would tell me exactly where I was. There would be no prospect of a cold bothyless night.

With no alternative but to trust my navigation, I head down into the glen, following the trembling compass needle, guided into the darkness by the invisible magnetic force. The moonlight flattens perspective, changes the appearance of the hills – there could be a cathedral here and I wouldn't be able to see it. Somehow there is always a small cloud covering the face of the moon. The cloud appears to be moving but it never goes anywhere. I need that moonlight now and look belligerently at the little wisp of star-brightened cloud that taunts me from far above. Suddenly Loch an Laoigh appears, grey and sparkling, like steel hammered flat, down in the glen. Now at least I know I'm in the right glen and I'll have a fixed point to work from if my compass bearing proves inadequate.

I stare again into the growing darkness but no bothy appears. Our urban lives have banished the night. In towns and cities it never really gets dark, but here, in this wild place, darkness gets off the lead and runs about unfettered.

Many years ago, when I first came to the Highlands with Joe and Mr Jones, we left the pub in Torridon at closing time to walk the mile or so back to our tent. Then, for the first time, I encountered real wild darkness: no street lights or car headlights, low cloud covering the moon and stars. We stumbled about unable to see each other or even the road, afraid of falling into the ditch. A drunken local in his Land Rover rescued us. Without him we might have had to crawl home. I never forgot to take a torch after that.

Ahead of me in the black I see a dark shape, there for a moment then gone. A few yards closer and my head torch picks out something solid and heavy but perhaps not the bothy. I stumble on until a gable end appears. I still daren't hope – this could be a ruin. Only when I can see the blue-painted door of the bothy, proof that I have found my home for the next two nights, do I relax.

That night is one of the coldest I've ever experienced in a bothy. The meagre fire makes little impression on the frost monster prowling about outside. I am forced to wear two hats whilst I watch Clint Eastwood tough it out, on my little tablet, though clouds of my own breath.

"Do you feel lucky, punk? Well do ya?"

The following day is bitterly cold. I explore the glen, wandering beside the loch and watching two swans on the water. It's too cold for the tops – but I'm glad, as it gives me time to enjoy such an isolated place. It's an odd business, sitting alone beside the semi-frozen water just watching the swans drift about. I want to get a sense of the silent, frozen glen and feel at peace just listening to the silence.

Walking along the water's edge I decide I wouldn't buy a GPS. I'd risk another night in the cold if I couldn't find a bothy again. If you rely solely on a map and compass you are in a much more intimate relationship with the landscape than if you use a location device. Of course, even map and compass are technology, just older and simpler than GPS. But there does seem to be something that separates you from where you are when you stare at a screen, and we spend so much of our lives these days doing just that. I'm no technophobe – after all, I watched a movie in the bothy, which ten years ago would have been all but impossible – but we have to get the balance right between new and old, between technology and nature. I'd be safer if I used a GPS and I'd always get to where I was going, but I think I'd have lost something from the journey and it's the journey that counts.

So, if one day when you are walking Scotland's hills, you see a cave man – club in hand and dressed in fur – chasing a deer, don't panic. It's only me, close to nature, making lunch.

A Quiet Word

What started as mist changed by degrees from fog to drizzle and then into a fine saturating rain. It is now what my mother would have called a 'wetting rain'; all rain is wet, but there is a fine mist of rain that laughs at Gore-Tex and will eventually find your skin no matter how well clad you are. This is that kind of rain and, by the last half mile of the walk to Shenavall, it is beginning to ooze through my gaiters and to seep up the sleeves of my cagoule. I am moistening at the edges, and not in a good way.

I reach the bothy and push open the white front door just in time to avoid a soaking. I know this door; in fact, I hung it a few years before on a Mountain Bothies Association work party. I'm glad to see it still fits and am happy that it closes behind me with a satisfying thud. It's dark in the bothy and I call out a quick hello into the gloom, looking forward to sitting beside the fire enjoying a few hours of company after the lonely walk.

A voice comes out of the darkness. "Oh, hello there. Would you like some tea?"

A large young man rushes to take my hand, a mop of tousled red hair framing his wide-browed face. He welcomes me enthusiastically into the small wood-lined room that reeks of woodsmoke, three-day-old socks and decaying food.

"I'm Hector," he says, pulling up a chair for me before

pouring a cup of tea.

The other two men beside the fire huddle closer as Hector offers his hospitality. The whites of their eyes flicker in the semi-darkness as they shoot me furtive, menacing glances. There is no mistaking the vehemence of the odd looks the two men give me. As I take my first sip of Hector's tea I wonder if these antisocial creatures treat all newcomers this way, or if there had been some disagreement about the best way to drink whisky or whether Ben Nevis would make an excellent site for a wind farm.

"Have you done all the Munros?" Hector asks breathlessly, and before I can answer he continues: "I've done ninety-three. The last one I did was Ben Nevis, terrible weather, rained all day. Took me five hours fifteen minutes to get to the top. And the one before that…"

He pins me to the wall with a torrent of words. He reels back through the hills he's climbed, telling me what the weather was like, how long it took him, what he had for lunch. Words pour in torrents from his mouth, far more powerful than anything the rain outside can produce. Ten minutes in, I can't hear what he's saying any more – I can just see his mouth moving as a jumble of insensible words rattle through my brain.

I cast a glance at the two men huddled in the corner. Now they are looking at me with sympathy and I realise that their menacing glances earlier were not threats but warnings.

"Now, number forty-three, you'll like this one," Hector rumbles on, unleashing an avalanche of words.

I wish I were at home or in another bothy. I don't care where I am as long as Hector isn't there. I wish he would be struck down by a catastrophic illness; then I wish he would die. I fantasise about how I will kill him. Smothering becomes my favoured option and I imagine his muffled words slowly ceasing as I force my sleeping bag into his mouth.

I look over at my other two companions muttering to each other in the corner. One glances up and we exchange a look of deep, dark despair. In that moment, I know that if I kill Hector – perhaps fell him with a blow from the cast-iron frying pan that hangs above the fire, drag him outside and bury him beneath the nettles – it would be a secret that I and my fellow Hector sufferers will carry to our graves. We will pass the rest of the evening in quiet, gentle conversation, knowing that there is no need to mention Hector's departure from this mortal realm. Each of us understanding that his removal, like disposing of a sheep tick in the groin, had simply been necessary.

Eventually, at about 8.30 – long after I have begun to wish I too were dead – it's agreed that it's bedtime. I settle in to my sleeping bag, content in the knowledge that now, at last, sleep will carry Hector off into the land of dreams and he will stop talking. Soon he falls silent and all I can hear is the sound of him gently snoring. The blessed silence lasts for around ten minutes and then, returning with all the joy of an unpaid tax bill, Hector's monotonous drone begins again. Robbed of the influence of his conscious mind, Hector's diatribe makes even less sense than it did when he was awake. The connection between his brain and his mouth is at best tenuous.

* * *

The following morning, we all go our separate ways. I try to push the lamentable evening to the back of my mind as I plod back to my car over the hills.

Driving back to my home in Inverness I spot a walker hitching by the side of the road. Without thinking I stop and the hiker climbs into the passenger seat. To my horror I realise it is Hector – I hadn't recognised him with his mouth closed. He explains that he is sure he is going to miss his train home from Inverness, as we are unlikely to get to the Highland capital before his train departs. Sadly, he tells me, he has nowhere to stay in Inverness if that happened and wonders if I might put him up for the night.

"Oh, don't worry," I tell him quietly. "I'm sure we'll get you to the station in time."

I am not by nature a fast driver, but I press the accelerator to the floor and keep it there for the whole journey. I drive as though I am pursued by the Devil, as though chased by every midge in the Highlands; I drive as though I am trying to catch last orders for end of time. Hector sits in the passenger seat, his white-knuckled fingers driven deep into the upholstery. Feet braced against the dashboard, his eyes are fixed on the road ahead, staring through the windscreen as though he can see Death driving a Forestry Commission lorry straight at us.

But, more importantly than all of that, he sits in total and complete silence.

First published on UKHillwalking.com

Requiem In Sutherland

Across the rolling moorland, close to the horizon, runs a man-made line. On this narrow strip of tarmac sits my car, a little black shape of manufactured steel in this Sutherland wilderness. The car looks tantalisingly close now. I imagine my tired legs carrying me the last few feet, visualise myself lowering my rucksack for the final time this day and sitting, at last, in the luxury of my patient, reliable vehicle.

I see all this in the same way a man in the desert holds a cool glass of clear water in his mind's eye. Driven by thirst the traveller watches the light dance in the liquid, feels the smooth cold of the glass in his hand; but all this is a dream, a mirage, an illusion. Just as the desert traveller may perish before he presses that cool glass to his lips, I begin to wonder if I'll ever reach the road.

* * *

It's a long while since I spent any time outdoors. This year has been full of long train journeys down to my father's home in Merseyside to sit with him while he grew weaker and age slowly gathered him in. He was 90 when the end came at last, in a hospital bed in Birkenhead, and that kind, gentle man, the giant of my childhood, slipped from this world like a leaf falling from a tree in autumn.

When he was too frail to walk abroad himself I would tell my father of my travels, the places I had been, things I had seen and the folk I met. He loved to see my pictures and liked, best of all, to see the images of bothy fires, imagining that he accompanied me on my remote wanderings, felt the warmth of the flames and breathed in the unsullied air.

It's been a while now since I picked up my rucksack and headed for open country. Far too long since I stood and watched the light fade on the hillside with no one but the whispering wind for company. This morning, as I stand beside the sea loch and watch the sea collide endlessly against the timeless cliffs, the peace of this place overwhelms me.

I have spent too long with my feet planted on man-made floors, and my eyes have grown tired of the world of straight lines and superimposed order. Too many hours in antiseptic hospital corridors amongst beeping instruments. Hours full of waiting, helplessness, hopelessness, and finally a gnawing, empty sadness.

As I stand on the shore amongst the chaos of boulders, the debris of long-forgotten storms, my eyes roam the ragged landscape and revel in the natural disorder. The hand of man is absent here. There are no roads or houses; for millenia, this place has been much as it is on this September day.

I need this place. I need to feel the wind against my skin and the sounds of the waves breaking and seabirds calling. The gentle wind tugs at the landscape and does something else to me: it blows away the tainted dust of the last few months, cleanses me of anguish.

Cleansed now and at ease with my surroundings, I walk

back to the simple stone shelter of the bothy. A simple meal of soup, bread and cheese seems like a feast, as only food can taste when eaten outdoors.

* * *

Usually it works like this. You walk in to a bothy laden with coal, food, whisky and other consumables. The heavy pack makes the walk in slow and tiring but on the way out, coal burnt, food eaten and whisky drunk, the pack is light and the going easy. This bothy is different. I left my car on the high road across the moors and descended over 600ft to the small bothy by the coast. Now I have to regain that height.

It's on the climb back to my car that the landscape of Sutherland reveals its secret weapon: bog. Here, at the northern fringe of Britain, there are trackless miles and miles of the stuff. Your feet sink in and every footfall has to be retrieved from the wet, sucking peat with a Herculean effort. The walk through the ooze feels endless. My legs are moving, I am sure of that, but I don't know if I am making any progress through the landscape. I stumble, lurch, fall and stagger but the car doesn't get any closer.

I try not to look up in case the lack of progress is too dispiriting but every now and again I give in to temptation. Sometimes it seems the vehicle is no closer; at other times it even seems to have moved further away. At last, legs quaking and lungs bursting, my boots hit the tarmac and I am able to move with a renewed freedom.

On the drive back to Inverness I realise that this trip has been different from all the others I have made; this time I will not show my photos to my father and tell him of my travels. I'll miss our times together but one thing consoles me. Last night, as I watched the flames flicker and the embers glow in the bothy fire, I felt as though he came and sat beside me and we enjoyed the dancing light together.

Black Norman's House

It's September in the Highlands and autumn has slipped, almost unnoticed, into the landscape. The season enters quietly, touching the leaves on the trees here and there with golden tinges. Outside the window of my flat, the sycamore trees are spotted yellow and a shiver of excitement runs through me. For mountain folk everywhere the arrival of autumn is exciting, for soon on this season's heels the hills will turn white and the great season, winter, will have begun. Our hills will be transformed from sleeping green mounds to ice-sheathed warriors – at least that's what I hope.

Autumn slinks in, stealthy and gentle, but always before she leaves she shakes this island of ours with the ferocity of a wolf attacking a sheep. By October, gales will sweep the land and hurl mountainous seas against our shores. I look forward to these extremes, to nights when I can sit in a bothy and hear the windows shake, feel the roof tremble as wind and rain hurl themselves at the defiant little shelter. I endure the summer; wait for it to leave, wait for the insects to perish and for the flocks of visitors to desert the hills and to leave the tea shops and hotels, to return to their quiet bumbling ways. Tourism is the lifeblood of the Highlands without which the place would wither and die. For me, however, a seeker of solitude, I am always pleased when the seasons turn and the summer is over.

It's no longer summer but not yet winter. Autumn in the Highlands is the in-between season, characterised by wind and rain, and my expeditions are often preceded by carefully studying weather maps, giving up in frustration and deciding to go and see what the weather does anyway. Sometimes I sit in my car watching the rain spattering on to the windscreen; at other times I'm treated to glorious days of sunshine and amazing colours as the seasons change in this northern landscape.

Last week, I was passing time on Facebook when I should have been writing. I read a post from the maintenance organiser of the remote bothy on Raasay, Taigh Thormoid Dhuibh, asking for information on the building's condition. I realised I'd never been there and decided that I'd make the trip. September was a good time, before the October storms and, hopefully, after the summer's midges. I'm semi-retired these days and have the freedom to make those kind of decisions; I can simply drop everything and go. I have amazing freedom and I am privileged in the ability to follow my heart whenever I want to. I haven't forgotten the hours I spent in meetings during my working days.

Taigh Thormoid Dhuibh, or Black Norman's House, sits on the northernmost tip of the long finger of Raasay which points to the Isle of Rona, separated from Raasay by a narrow strip of water known as a 'kyle'. It's Monday afternoon when I drive from Inverness to the Isle of Skye and make my way to where the little ferry shuttles back and forth between Skye and Raasay, a journey of 25 minutes. Less than 200 folk live on Raasay, although the island's population rises in the summer and a new distillery may bring a few more people to this far-flung place.

The island is long and narrow and most of its population is clustered around the ferry terminal. From afar, if the island is not completely shrouded in mist as it often is for months of the year, the extinct volcano of Dun Caan dominates the view with its distinctive conical shape and flat top. The view from the summit is said to be exceptional although I can't testify to this myself. If you are looking for fine views on the Isle of Skye I can recommend Beinn na Caillich, a small hill that sits above the village of Broadford. It's a relatively short climb to the summit, where legend says a fairy princess is buried. There is a fantastic panorama of Skye which is ample reward for the climb.

I head north and, after a few miles, find myself on the famous Callum's Road. This is not a place to cruise along admiring the scenery. I travel with my eyes glued to the narrow strip of tarmac in front as it takes me down alarming slopes, twisting around bends that leave me hovering precariously over steep drops to the sea.

Calum MacLeod, a resident of North Raasay and the local lighthouse keeper and postman, campaigned for years to get the council to build the road – but to no avail. Not to be dissuaded, he built the road himself with a pick, a shovel, and a little assistance from some dynamite. The feat took him some ten years, starting in 1964. In the end, the council gave in and adopted the road so it is now a public road, although not one for the faint hearted. It doesn't go anywhere in particular and certainly not as far as the bothy so, as I laced up my boots, I had some four miles to walk to the tip of Raasay to find the little shelter.

There are times when I begin to despair as I'm walking to a bothy, and this walk on Raasay is one of them. I think I should be there by now as my feet sink in to the bog for the thousandth time and my pack, with its supply of coal, grows heavier with every step. Highland bothies have a way of toying with the unsuspecting traveller. They hide from him, make him doubt his bearings, wonder if he has walked past the place. I'm walking north and I am beginning to run out of island when, at last, the bothy pops up from behind a hillock, jeering at me like an errant schoolboy playing hide and seek. It was here all the time.

The bothy is a simple, one-room affair with a sleeping platform at one end and a ramshackle hearth at the other. I'm grateful for its shelter as I unpack my sleeping bag and prepare a meal, which I devour in minutes. The fire lights with little difficulty but smoke belches from the hearth and fills the bothy. Now my eyes smart and I can't see the far end of the room. Every few minutes, I open the door to release the smoke until the chimney heats up enough to draw the smoke out and I can relax before the fire.

As night falls, small pinpricks of light begin to emerge against the dark hills of the Isle of Skye across the Sound of Raasay. The Vikings called Skye 'The Winged Isle', reflecting its shape jutting into the Atlantic. I lived on Skye for seven years where I worked as a social worker and my time there was an education. Islands are very different places from anywhere on the mainland of Scotland; they all have their personalities. Orkney is vastly different from the Western Isles, and Skye differs from the others. There is an attitude on the island, a philosophy of life, that the newcomer has to adjust to.

My first education in this attitude came when I needed a tradesman to fix our garage door. The local joiner informed me he would be round 'next Tuesday' to do the job. Tuesday came but no joiner. I phoned him again, on several occasions; he promised he would come but never did. I realised I had made an elementary mistake: I had assumed that next Tuesday was a date, a point in time. It is not. It is a concept. 'Next Tuesday' means that the joiner may come at some undetermined date in the future, or he may *never* come. 'Next Tuesday' means that everything and anything may, and probably will be, put off to some time in the future when it won't need to be done at all. If you wait long enough, nothing matters – empires fall, mountains crumble, garage doors rattle on broken hinges until they eventually fall off and blow away.

On another occasion, the lock on our office door refused to function. I called out the council joiner who – presumably having nothing better to do – showed up, worked for an hour on the door, then packed up his tools and made to leave.

I tried the door and the lock didn't function. "This door still doesn't lock."

He looked at me with an expression of infinite sadness, as if I were a poor lost soul burdened with irrelevant worries. "Ah, yes. Yes, yes, you're right there. But you see, it's not as bad as it was before."

For years, the cafe in the square at Portree, Skye's main town, closed at lunchtime so the staff could enjoy their meals, leaving tourists and locals alike hungry in the rain. It is a lifestyle dictated by the need to bring everything from the mainland. Skye is a place where delays are not frustrations but opportunities to enjoy life – perhaps a philosophy we could all learn from.

In the morning, I pack up my smoke-infused sleeping bag and gear and take some photos so that the Maintenance Organiser of the bothy would be able to plan the next work party. Priority number one has to be a better fireplace.

I walk out through drizzle and mist and drive back, along Calum's twisty road, to the ferry terminal. After an hour, the ferry comes into view and disgorges its cars and passengers onto the slipway. I start my car and prepare to board when, to my surprise, the vehicle ramp is raised and the ferry shuts down.

"What's going on?" I ask a local, smoking against the terminal wall.

He belches smoke into the breeze. "Oh, the ferry isn't leaving now. Yes, yes, yes. The crew are having their lunch hour."

Well, of course they are; what's the hurry?

Never On Sunday

It's Sunday morning in Glenbrittle campsite at the foot of the Cuillin hills on the Isle of Skye. Daylight seeps through the walls of my tent but I try to ignore it and wriggle down into the warm cocoon of my sleeping bag. The first thing I do is feel my legs. Sure enough, they remember yesterday's climb and respond sluggishly, letting me know that they would like another couple of hours' sleep in an 'if you think we're taking you up there again today you've another thing coming' sort of a way. Reluctantly I free an arm from the confines of my sleeping bag. As I unzip a tiny portion of the door my head recalls last night's beer in the Sligachan and joins my legs in pleading for slumber.

They need not have worried. Outside the air is thick with a mixture of drizzle and midges and it takes me a millisecond to agree with both ends of my anatomy and decide that today is a 'rest day'. All around me other members of the mountaineering club are stirring and all are reaching the same conclusion.

Then I hear it: Ting! Ting! Ting! I can only see the rear sealed end of the tent next door but I know what's going on.

Ting! Ting! Ting! The unmistakable sound of a Primus stove being charged with pressure.

"Where's the bloody matches?" comes Davey's deep Aberdonian drawl from inside his canvas abode.

"I'm reading." That's Pat, his elf-like, red-headed wife, curled up with a book in the door of the tent.

"Aye, here they are."

Scratch, scratch, scratch, Davey's bear-like paws are fumbling with the Swan vestas. Then it comes, a faint 'boof' followed by the roar of the Primus coming to life and the rattle of the kettle going onto the stove.

"Keep an eye on the stove will ya?"

"I'm reading."

I'm scanning the horizon, reassuring myself that the Cuillins are snoozing comfortably under a blanket of wet clouds, when I hear: "Pat! Pat!"

"I'm reading."

Pat, a lover of detective novels, is far away in the back streets of New York, desperate to see if Scarface is about to get caught by the Boothill mob and take the big sleep. It's at this point I hear a strange tearing sound. Until now, the morning has been filled with the familiar domestic sounds of the waking campsite and every little noise has betrayed the activities of my tented neighbours.

I peer over at Davey and Pat's tent and notice a little silver shape, like a shark's fin, slicing down the surface of the canvas. It takes me a moment to grasp that it's the blade of Davey's Swiss army knife. Then Davey's moustached head appears, followed by his broad shoulders. He struggles through the sliced canvas and stands for a moment staring at the tent as if he's forgotten something. I'm trying to work out why he didn't use the door at the front when he lurches back through the makeshift opening only to emerge clutching his sleeping bag which, to his evident consternation, is smouldering. Davey runs about frantically trying to extinguish it, filling the air with smoke and feathers, only becoming calm when he is clearly satisfied that all is well with his bag.

Pat's voice cuts through the air of the sleepy campsite – "Oh my God!" – and she comes flying through the hole in the back of the tent like a jet-propelled fairy.

It's then that I notice flames beginning to leap up from the door of Pat and Davey's tent. Pandemonium breaks out. Moments later I'm running about in my underpants trying to fetch water. Other club members are also hurling not only water but tea and porridge – anything wet – at the rising flames.

In the struggle between tent and fire, however, there can only be one winner, and within minutes we are all standing, gazing forlornly, at a rectangle of charred grass marking the spot where the couple's temporary home had stood minutes before. There's one thing I've learned over the years about paraffin stoves: you can't trust them. One moment they are purring away, nice as pie, warming your soup; then you turn your back and they flare up and make a lunge for the roof of your tent, giggling like a gremlin.

Pat's book lies black and smoking in the ashes. I silently hand it to her. She takes it disconsolately, turning it over, and it is obvious that the last few chapters have been lost to the flames. "Och, now I'll never know who rubbed out Chalky," she declares, and I can see a thought passing through her mind. Furious, she turns to Davey. "Why didn't you drag me out the tent instead of that bloody bag?"

Davey is hurt, as though the question is too ridiculous. "This is a damn good sleeping bag, these are hard to get!" Then he adds, "You can always get another wife."

The Cherry Tree

The world is full of giants. They lumber about me, and I, at four years old, scamper between their legs waiting for the occasional face to peer down or a hand to appear bearing a Quality Street chocolate. The green triangular ones are the best and I unwrap these treasures with reverence before savouring their delicious velveteen centres.

Beside the tin fishing hut that I visit with my father every Sunday grows a tiny cherry tree, little more than a sapling. Small though I am, if I press my thumbs together I can place my palms against the silvery bark and just touch my fingertips together on the far side of the tree. Sometimes I stand like this for a few minutes, listening to the leaves rustling in the wind and feeling the tree sway, fascinated by the enormity of the fact that I am big enough to hold a tree in my hands.

The land of my Merseyside home is rich in clay. In Victorian times men would arrive in the fields with horses pulling carts and begin to dig. Their goal was beneath the soil: the clay which they would cart away to make bricks for the terraced houses of the industrial workers who toil in the shipyards of Birkenhead. These clay pits were soon abandoned and in time they filled with water, trees grew around them, and they were populated by fish, water voles and aquatic plants. My father is a member of a small club, the Wirral Angling Association. When not working as a shipping clerk, he spends most of his free time fishing at the ponds.

As a small boy I roam around the ponds, exploring the trees and bushes, walking across the precarious wooden bridges that lead out onto islands or small pontoons. Here I battle space monsters, have shoot-outs with many foes and follow the vivid footsteps of my imagination. Gradually my father introduces me to his world, shows me the whirligig beetles and water boatmen – tiny insects who spend their lives rushing across the meniscus of the water, miraculously balanced on the surface tension. The whirligig beetles race in circles across the water pursued by the water boatmen who look like tiny oarsmen in miniature boats.

My father shows me the criss-crossed tracks left by water voles, mice and other creatures. These little pathways fascinate me and I spend hours following them and wondering which animals made them. Merseyside is a crowded place, crammed with people, industry and intensive agriculture. The River Mersey is so polluted it is toxic to life and even capable of bursting into flames. Around these few ponds, however, in a small, sometimes near-microscopic world, my father and I cling to these outposts of nature surrounded by a man-made jungle.

Beneath the water there lies a secret world full of myriad lives. Some days, when there is enough sunshine, I climb a tree and look down into the water from above. On days like these I watch as underwater shapes rise from the depths. I see bulbous carp basking below the surface and feeding beneath the lily pads. Shoals of silvery roach flit between the shelter of weed beds in cloud-like formations. Sometimes my pulse quickens when I see the long, streamlined shape of a pike floating motionless amongst the weeds waiting for a careless roach to swim too close. When a fish comes within range, the pike – the striped tiger of these waters – explodes with lightning speed through the water and closes its many-toothed jaws about its hapless prey.

My father's only method of transportation is an old sturdy bicycle. He is unable to afford motorised transport on a clerk's wage. As a child I climb onto a small seat on the back and, with me on board, he cycles the three miles to the waters of the angling club. As I get bigger he teaches me the art of angling. We spend hours watching the quills of the floats he has made from birds' feathers sit motionless in the water. The only fish of any size are tench, slimy green bottom-feeders, but even these are rarely caught.

When it rains or becomes too cold we retreat to the shelter of a few wooden huts that keep away the winter winds. The huts are full of fishing rods and nets. They smell of damp and the paraffin that leaks from the stoves that my father lights to offer some warmth. In the dim light of the huts, when the weather is foul, we sit together with a few old men who have been fishing here for over twenty years. As the heat from the stoves rises from beneath the table the old men sit, drinking tea and swapping stories of the great fish that they believe lurk somewhere beneath the murky waters. The roof of the tin hut reverberates to falling acorns and the rattle of twigs.

In the summer we rise early and walk across the meadows laced with a million spider's webs sparkling in the early morning dew. The hours just after dawn are magical times, caught in the moment before the world wakes when it is easy to believe that we are alone. After hours of fishing, we return to the hut and feast on sausages and the mushrooms we pick along the way. Anyone who has eaten in the outdoors will know that there is no taste richer than a meal eaten in the fresh air and spiced by hunger.

In the winter, when the icy wind blows, we build fires in old oil drums to warm our hands whilst fishing for the elusive pike. Short winter days and cold winds give these days a spice I grow to relish. Once in a while, even on mild Merseyside, temperatures sink low enough and long enough for the ponds to freeze over. Even then, with all pretence at fishing gone, we spend our weekends walking around the ponds and marvel at the ice crystals and the changed, white landscape.

My father died last year at the age of 90, only months after catching his last fish in those ponds. That gentle man had spent over 70 years beside those waters. They had been his companion, his source of peace, a place away from the pressures of life. He had a connection with those few acres of land that is rare in the modern world – and something precious.

It has taken me many years to realise that the sense of belonging I feel when sitting in a Highland bothy comes from those days, many years ago, when I sat in that fishing hut listening to the acorns bouncing off the roof. Even today, as I walk in to bothies, the habits he planted in me persist. I find myself scouring the ground for the tracks of animals. In nights beside the bothy fire part of me is still a boy surrounded by giants.

If you go to those ponds now, you will see that the cherry tree still grows beside the hut. It is mature now and even my adult hands can reach only halfway around its trunk. It is more than fifty years since I first held that tree in the palms of my hands. Half a lifetime has passed by. Perhaps that cherry tree will live another fifty years, in a time when no one will remember the small boy who placed his hands around its trunk.

King Of Kearvaig

The light is fading quickly. Above the silhouettes of the low hills a weak moon peers through fleeting clouds. I have been walking for several hours now and my pack, crammed with sleeping bag, coal, food and whisky, is rapidly growing heavier and making an increasing impression on my shoulders. It's February and night has crept up on me. I am reduced to following the dwindling circle of light cast by my torch on the empty tarmac road.

I am heading for a bothy whose name has long lingered in my imagination and which has finally drawn me through the remote lochs and glens of Sutherland. I'm about as far north as it is possible to go without tumbling off mainland Britain and falling headlong into the ocean. I'm heading for Kearvaig, one of the most remote bothies on mainland Britain.

Coming here had seemed a great idea when I was sitting in my centrally heated flat in Inverness. Now, as the chill wind rises and tickles my skin with the occasional snowflake, I am beginning to wonder if I had been entirely wise to embark on this trip. When I pause to consult my map, it occurs to me that I am probably the most remote person in Britain. It is twelve miles to the nearest house and the road I am standing on gives a false impression of a link to civilisation. One end of the road is only accessible by boat across the Kyle of Durness and the other ends at the Cape Wrath lighthouse, an isolated beacon warning seafarers of the jagged rocks that mark the north-westernmost corner of mainland Britain.

It's at moments like these that my decision to travel alone quickens my mind and brings the experience of isolation into sharp focus. If I had company we'd be arguing about how far we had to go and which route to take, focused more on the debate than on the landscape. Alone in this place, I have no one else to rely on, no one to fall back on if the going gets tough. Getting to this bothy depends solely on me, my judgement and my fitness. That is how I like it.

From the sea inlet of the Kyle of Durness, a four-mile tear in the coastline, the narrow tarmac road I have been following makes its way across the rolling moorland populated by sheep and deer. In the darkness it is not always easy to pinpoint my position but eventually I arrive at a junction where a track leads away from the tarmac towards a bay with the bothy nestling beneath the cliffs (or so I hope). The problem at night is that one track looks very much like another and I am cautious of leaving the tarmac in case I have mistaken the track and find myself lost in the darkness. It's then that I notice a little shed sitting incongruously at the junction. When I lean against the door it bursts open and I find it full of tins of paint and rolls of barbed wire. Here, I decide, is my backup plan. The shed has no stove or fireplace but it is windproof and dry; if I descend this track and find no bothy at the end of it I can at least find some shelter for the night.

As I descend the track in the blackness the air begins to fill with the smell of the sea and I hear the rhythmic pounding of the breaking waves, distant at first and then closer as I approach the shore. Pebbles begin to crunch beneath my feet and the smell of the sea fills my nostrils as I seek out this secret place. Still my head-torch beam finds nothing but the emptiness of the night until a white shape looms out of the blackness and a moment later I am pushing open the door.

In the summer months, Kearvaig is less remote; a boat plies back and forth across the mile of sea and meets a minibus that shuttles between the little pier and the white tower of the lighthouse. Tourists, bedecked with cameras, sun hats and shorts, trundle towards Cape Wrath and bask for a while in the knowledge that they made it to the north-westernmost point on the mainland. A few even make the minor detour to visit the bothy so, for few brief months, Kearvaig enjoys a little time in the sun as a celebrity bothy. Come winter, everything changes. The ferry ceases and the minibus no longer plies its trade across the moorland. It is then that Kearvaig returns to its isolation and becomes, once again, one of the most inaccessible dwellings on mainland Britain.

If the waters of the Kyle and the miles of moorland, exposed to the full force of the Atlantic weather, were not enough of a barrier to the casual visitors, Kearvaig has a secret weapon in its attempt to repel boarders. If you go at the wrong time you'll get blown up.

I had spent a couple of hours prior to my visit hunting down numbers on the internet and finally had to resort to phoning the RAF. A very nice young lady answered the phone and took infinite trouble to find out whether I would be fired on whilst crossing the moor to Kearvaig. The moorland is a firing range and is, periodically, used by our military to discharge all sorts of vicious munitions that could render the assaults of weather and midges alike on the weary traveller superfluous.

Evidence of Kearvaig's military role is apparent when you pass through a checkpoint, complete with chequered flag and movable barrier. Fortunately, the sentry box was empty when I passed by and only a few sheep noticed me passing the empty houses at the beginning of the road. I make no secret of the fact that I'm opposed to the increasing trend of the tidy-minded to place signs on Britain's hills. At the end of many roads that reach into the hills are signs, placed there by the irrepressibly helpful to guide those of us who would otherwise wander lost. These signs point to distant places sometimes over fifteen miles away. I am mystified by the reasoning behind such signs. If they are for folk who can't navigate they are useless unless the whole route is signposted. If you can navigate you don't need them; if you can't they are no use.

Best of all are the warning signs that don't point anywhere but simply say 'Careful now, there are mountains about'. Well all right they don't actually say that; they say things like 'You are entering mountainous terrain'. That isn't very helpful, is it? They should put up signs that say 'It's a long way to the next McDonald's' or 'You won't get a decent latte round here'.

In stark contrast to signs elsewhere, the walk in to Kearvaig boasts some of the best signs you'll ever come across. They have signs like, 'Don't step off the road, danger of explosion and death'. That's the kind of sign I like; there's a piece of information I can use. The whole place is littered with unexploded munitions so wandering about off road is best discouraged. Walking in the moonlight in that isolated spot I was very grateful of any sign that told me how to keep my arms and legs attached.

The fire is slow to catch, but eventually I coax flames up the chimney until it spits out at me like an old man reluctant to rise from his sleep. It had been two months since a few RAF personnel had taken the rough boggy walk in from the south, and toasted in the new year before the very fire that was now warming the ache out of my legs.

The bothy is surprisingly spacious with several rooms downstairs and a few habitable rooms on the first floor. I took the room with the best-looking fireplace and soon settled in with my basic bothy food, pausing only to set up my bed. Now, meal eaten, I have only to sit and watch the flames dance for the evening in perfect solitude far from the cares of the everyday world. I sit dozing that night in the rough-hewn armchair some visitor had constructed to pass the time many months before. Perhaps thinking it like a throne, another hand had etched across the back of the seat the words 'King of Kearvaig'.

Kearvaig has not always been a happy place. In the winter of 2002 an unfortunate visitor starved to death here. Margaret Davies was 39 when, in October or November, she travelled to this far outpost of Britain in search of solitude. At that time of year solitude is one of the few things Kearvaig has in abundance. Little is known of what befell her at the bothy, but she must have spent weeks there before two shepherds noticed the bothy door was open and became concerned – an open door at that time of year is unusual. It was the 5th of December.

They found the poor woman emaciated and semi-conscious in her sleeping bag. In the window of the bothy was a desperate note left for passers-by, offering to pay for food. Sadly no one passes by Kearvaig at that time of year. She was flown to hospital, but her condition had deteriorated too far and she passed away a few days later.

What exactly happened is a mystery. It's clear that this poor woman was an experienced, fit hiker, having undertaken treks in the Himalayas. Oddly, no one in the villages nearby remembered seeing her although she must have passed through at least one on the journey to the bothy. She had been well equipped at the outset although eventually began to run low on food. I read that there had been a flu epidemic in the area around the time that this woman had been there, and I can only surmise that this may have played a part. It's possible that, after contracting the virus, she was too weak to make the strenuous trek – or perhaps attempted to get out and was driven back by exhaustion and bad weather. If that is the case, then the exertion of trying to extract herself from the situation would have severely depleted what little reserves she had left and could have led to a rapid deterioration. It is such a shame that this magical place has been marred by tragedy.

I wake to the rhythmic sound of breakers crashing onto the shingle of the beach as they have done for millennia. The weather is kind for February and I wander across the bay, watching the greenish blue breakers rolling endlessly, driven by the power of the Atlantic. Here, so far north and west, I gaze out towards the distant horizon knowing that beyond the point where the sky and the water meet in an endless line there is nothing but waves between me and the Americas. Winter sunshine picks out the outline of the cliffs surrounding the small bay. Steep cliffs fall into the sea, dark and foreboding, great clouds of spray rising as the waves pound into them.

Time has not touched this place. It looks much the same as it did when the last ice age receded, when the Vikings brought terror to these coasts, or when British battleships scoured the Atlantic in search of their German foe. It is 8.30 a.m. as I walk along the shore in this enchanted place. In London, commuters are wedging themselves into sweaty tube trains and bracing themselves for another day in the office. All across the UK people are sitting in traffic jams, punching clocks or switching on computer screens, getting ready for the tedium of another day. Yet here I am, with only the seabirds for company and the vast ocean; I am indeed King of Kearvaig.

The Yellow-Eyed Bird Of Glen Dubh-Lighe

The big man grunted as he drove the shovel into the earth, his breath misting in the cold winter air. His two companions watched the spade rise and fall as the mound of soil grew. They stood beside the pile of earth – one stocky and bald, the other a thin and mouse-like creature with a black hat crammed onto his head. Every few moments the small man's gaze would dart into the surrounding forest and he would scan the snow-covered fir trees in the steep-sided valley. He searched uncertain of what he might find but fearful of anything that might be watching him from the dark of the woodland.

At last the big man, sweating and blowing from his efforts, stepped back from the heap of dark earth and drove the spade into the ground with an unmistakable finality. The three stood in silence for a moment staring forlornly at his handiwork.

"Perhaps," the small man stammered, "we should say a few words." There was a pause as each man looked to the others to speak. "John, you're good with words, you say something."

John spat onto the ground, zipped up his red jacket as the wind had suddenly grown cold, and turned to the wee man. "Nigel, what's done is done. We can't change anything with words." Then John grew sombre and drew the little group about him. "We must never speak of this to our dying days. Not a word to anyone."

Nigel whimpered a little but nodded in assent. The big man said nothing and John turned to him, grasped his sweat-stained waterproof, and drew him near. "Not a word, Kev. We've done a terrible thing."

Big Kev shrugged. "Aye, a ken fine." His face was wet from sweat and the melting snowflakes that were falling in ever-increasing flurries, beading in his grey curly hair.

"What did he say?" Nigel asked in his shrill south-of-England accent.

John turned and began walking back to the bothy. "He'll say nothing," he called over his shoulder. "I think we all need a brew."

As the three men walked slowly back to the bothy the glen fell back into silence, save for the wind tugging at the tops of the pines and water babbling in the half-frozen river. The scene was as it had been for countless years past: Glen Dubh-Lighe, deep and quiet, hidden from the world, a place of winter frosts and summer rains, a tranquil gentle place save for one small thing. Save for the little mound of earth and its dark secret.

* * *

The seeds of what happened that morning had been planted in the dark of the night before. John had been dozing before the bothy fire, a generous mug of whisky balanced on his paunch, when the door had rattled open. Nigel walked in from the black, wet night and stood for a moment, melting snow dripping onto the wooden floor.

"Nice bothy," Nigel had said by way of greeting, his eyes taking in the woodwork of the bothy walls gleaming in the candlelight. "Shiny!"

John stirred from his slumbers as he became aware of the soggy figure in the doorway. He rose to meet him as one might an honoured guest; after all the night would be long and dark and here was some welcome company.

"A dram?" John extended an arm to proffer a battered aluminium bottle, the veteran of many nights of lawless revelry.

Nigel drew back as though John's fingers held a belligerent rattlesnake. "Oh no, I don't thank you." He grinned apologetically, sensing that this was not the reply the bothy dweller had been hoping for. "And besides, tomorrow I'm off up the hills. I calculate two hours forty-five minutes to the summit. I'll need a clear head for that, you know."

John turned back towards the fire and stared hard into the glowing embers. He had little time for teetotallers and even less for those who plodded the hills to rigid schedules.

The small man's voice cut in to John's thoughts once more. "Which way will you be going up tomorrow? I think the east ridge is probably the quickest, but then the west ridge might give better views."

"Oh Christ!" he muttered to himself. The night had just grown darker and longer still. He picked up the poker and rammed it with venom into the glowing coal.

Nigel busied himself unpacking his neatly folded clothes from his rucksack an uncomfortable silence slowly filling the little shelter. "I heard this bothy burnt down a few years ago, accident with a gas canister."

John laughed as he stirred the fire, his back to the room. "That's what they tell everyone. That's the story the Mountain Bothies Association made up. Truth is it was burnt down by a jealous woman who caught her lover here having a secret fling with another woman."

At that moment a light flashed across the bothy window from outside. Seconds later something bear-like followed the light and the two men in the small room heard the sound of the outer door bursting open. This was followed by something heavy colliding with the walls until, finally, the door of their inner sanctum flew open. A figure filled the doorway. It was a man, but a huge individual. He bent himself almost double in an effort to heave himself through and, although he got most of his body through, his massive backpack wedged itself firmly in the opening.

Nigel cowered in a corner. John would have fled too but the whisky was beginning to take effect and he was having difficulty rising. The visitor moaned in frustration and heaved against the door, letting out a string of unintelligible oaths in a guttural tongue that could only be Aberdonian. The huge figure heaved again and, just when it seemed he might burst the doorway apart, he hurtled into the room followed closely by his massive pack.

The grey-suited figure stood grinning for a moment and said, "Muckle fir ma backpack twa yon door, ya ken."

This was probably some kind of greeting for, despite his ominous size, the giant looked amiable enough. He unbuckled his pack. Freed from its bonds, it hurtled into the floorboards with a sickening crunch that made the whole bothy shudder.

Gleefully the behemoth plunged into his rucksack and began pulling out tins of beer, bottles of wine, a whole ham, a cold chicken, and a gigantic sack of coal that he dumped beside the fire.

Muttering to himself, he thrust a can of beer into John's hands and another into Nigel's before opening one himself and downing it in several enormous gulps. Nigel cleared his throat – no doubt about to make his two hours and forty-five minutes speech – but he looked up at the creature towering over him and closed his mouth again, perhaps deciding that a few sips were unlikely to prove as dangerous as spurning the proffered hospitality.

It soon became clear that the newcomer could understand whatever was said to him even if his responses sounded like the last gasps of a drowning man. The colossus answered to the name Big Kev. This may not have been his name but it sufficed to get his attention so no further enquiries into the man's identity were needed.

The night progressed as many do in lonely bothies in the hills. The fire grew higher as Big Kev waded through his inexhaustible supply of beer. Communication was limited but they got by with sign language and mime, the small Englishman giving a very passable imitation of a chicken being roasted over a fire when John asked him what flavour crisps he was eating.

Nigel began meticulously folding out his spare clothing into neat piles, watched by Kev and John as the piles grew higher and it became evident that he was prepared for every foreseeable eventuality (and a few that couldn't be foreseen). Satisfied with his preparations, Nigel turned to John.

"So, where's it to be tomorrow?"

"I might just walk up the glen," John said, "take a look at the corrie. I'll see how I feel."

"Now if I were you," Nigel began, "I'd walk up onto the ridge. Only take you an hour and you'll get fine views from there."

"I'll see how I feel tomorrow."

"You could walk to the summit from there in about one hour thirty," Nigel persisted.

John was growing irritated at the Englishman's attempts to organise him. "I might not want to go to the top."

"Not want to go to the top? But you have to—"

John exploded. "I'll go where I bloody well want!"

There was an awkward silence and Nigel excused himself for a moment to go outside into the snow and rid himself of the beer Big Kev had pressed on him. The pair who remained were silently warming their legs by the glowing embers when Nigel burst back into the room.

"There's something out there!" he cried, the snowflakes from the blizzard outside melting on his jacket. "I saw a pair of yellow eyes watching me from the forest."

Outside, the trio raked the darkness with their head torches but saw only the falling snow and the ranked trees of the forest. "Nothing," Nigel stammered. "I heard it, it went beep beep."

"Beep, beep, Nigel!" John winked at Big Kev. "That settles it. You must have seen the Yellow-Eyed Bird of Glen Dubh-Lighe!"

Back in the bothy, Nigel's objections to drinking whisky were dispelled by his encounter with the bird and he held his mug in trembling hands as he swallowed the fiery liquid. "I've never heard of this Yellow-Eyed Bird before."

"It's not talked about, kept a secret by those who know," John explained as Big Kev stifled a chuckle. "Prehistoric, you see, like the monster of Loch Ness. If word got out, the glen would become a tourist attraction and we wouldn't want that."

They fell to talking about monsters and creatures that walk in the night and after a while forgot all about the bird that Nigel had seen. Forgot, that is, until Big Kev glanced at the window and his eyes grew wide with fear.

"Ach a boodie!"

There, pressed hard against the icy window pane, were two yellow eyes peering into the bothy. All three men froze as the creature turned and headed for the door. There was the chilling sound of the front door being opened and then something moving down the short corridor towards the room where they sat.

"Beep, beep," came the call and the door swung open.

Into the room came a thing made of metal, two glowing yellow lights on its head and, between them, a round cold-eyed camera lens. Nigel scrambled into the corner behind the coal bucket. John leapt from his chair and hurled his fist at the thing. The blow would have killed anything it hit but the whisky and beer had taken their toll and the punch arched wildly through the air, missing the alien thing by a foot or more. The momentum carried the inebriate round and he collapsed to the floor, overturning the bothy table on his way down; he found himself battered by an avalanche of pots and pans, candles and beer cans.

The creature took all of this in with its artificial eye. It saw Nigel attempting to make himself invisible. It saw John struggling to extricate himself from beneath the mountain of bothy dwellers' accoutrements. It saw the fire and the candles and the overturned chairs, but it did not see everything – it did not see Big Kev behind the door with the toilet spade raised over his head. It did not see him step out of the shadows and summon all his strength for the blow.

The men stood in silence staring at the little robot. It made no sound but shuddered slightly as sparks flickered where its ears might have been. Smoke drifted out from its carcass before the yellow lights in its head flickered and died. Then all was quiet as the creature stood in the bothy, cold and silent, a great flat dent in its head just above the words painted in yellow: 'GOOGLE BOTHY'.

So now if you walk up the little glen over the rickety wooden bridge to where the bothy stands, and make your way down towards the river, you will find a small mound of earth that looks somehow out of place. And if the wind is still, and the burn low and quiet, you can press your ear against the incongruous mound. If you do all that, you may just hear, so quiet you might think it your imagination, a muffled "Beep, beep". For that is all that remains of the Yellow-Eyed Bird of Glen Dubh-Lighe.

From My Cold Dead Hand

The path begins to descend through the forest and that just doesn't feel right. I stand looking at the map again and can see no such descent. It occurs to me that I've passed the bothy, so I begin to backtrack. Now I find paths weaving in and out of the woodland, none of which appears on my map.

After about an hour of fruitless searching in the darkness I turn around and head out of the forest, back to my car three miles away. Once out of the forest there's enough moonlight for me to walk without my head torch. I'm more than a little frustrated by my failure to find the bothy but as I walk back to the car something strange happens: I realise I'm enjoying myself.

The glen is wild and empty. Great clouds sweep across the sky, their huge shapes picked out by the glow of the moon. The low hills are brushed with early winter snow and seem friendly rather than remote. The wind picks up in the open glen and catches me in brief flurries of spindrift. I revel in being alone in this place far from technology and the clamour and chatter of the 21st century.

As I drive back through Aviemore to my home in Inverness I consider again my stubborn refusal to use a GPS device, relying on the more primitive technology of map and compass.

If I'd given in to the temptation to purchase one of these digital miracles I would be sitting in the bothy just now, instead of driving back home reflecting on my own incompetence. Perhaps it's time to give in and link myself to the guidance of celestial beings that can ease my passage through any maze of pine and fir.

Then I come to a decision: I'd rather die than use GPS. Here's why.

In a handful of years it will be possible to get a phone signal anywhere in the UK – that's everywhere from Corrour bothy in the heart of the Cairngorms to Cape Wrath in the far north, from Snowdonia to the cliffs of Great Gable. It will never be possible to be alone again and something will have changed forever. Wherever you are, the great seething mass of cyber-linked chattering irrelevance will be able to seek you out. Turning off your phone or even – perish the thought – leaving it at home will not be an option, for mountain-goers who do so will be branded reckless and foolhardy. The *Daily Mail* will tip that great cauldron of scorn (which they keep hot for such an occasion) down upon you with a righteous indignation they normally reserve for the tightness of Russell Brand's trousers.

Insurance companies will refuse to pay out on the demise of phone non-users. They have every right so to do; after all, rescue and divine guidance are readily available with a twitch of the thumb. To ignore such life-saving assistance is close to suicidal. Charles from the office will give you a quick call as you step into Tower Gap, one icy February day, to remind you that the sales figures for last month are due in tomorrow. Everyone will be expected to be available all the time everywhere. In this risk-averse society, those shrugging off the digital duvet will become outcasts and lepers.

That, of course, is only the beginning. Here's the future:

As Andy steps onto the Cairngorm plateau the microchip in his helmet fires into life. "Warning, snowstorm approaching, arrival twenty-three minutes," says the female voice of his communication centre in gentle, reassuring tones as if she were announcing the delivery of hot buttered toast. An image flashes up on his visor displaying an animated weather map where a swirling cloud of snow advances towards him in little bytes of time.

"Hazard approaching. Risk of fatal gravitational incident." Another map appears on the visor. This time the ice-coated cliffs of the corrie are highlighted red. Despite these adverse conditions Andy is one of the more adventurous of his generation, having once ridden a bicycle off road, and decides to carry on, pausing only to turn up the temperature control on his heated jacket. As he approaches the summit, Andy's visor flashes up reminders for insurance companies, a young lady explains to him how his clothes could come cleaner in the wash, and a takeaway company promises to deliver pizzas of unimaginable deliciousness to his home in moments. Andy decides he'll pay the extra subscription next time and get the advert-free version of the guidance device. From the summit the plateau stretches away white as icing sugar and twice as inviting. Despite the flashing arrow guiding him home, Andy decides to press on.

"Deviation alert," intones the young woman. "You have departed from your authorised route."

Andy strides on, enjoying the freedom and looking in awe at the snow-covered peaks of the Cairngorms. The young woman whispering in his ear grows ever more insistent that he must return to his agreed route, pointing out that Andy lacks the experience credits necessary to continue.

At last, in a reckless fury, Andy rips the visor from his face and stands alone on the snow as the sky darkens and ice crystals drift down from the snow-filled heavens to melt on his exposed skin. As he does so one last phrase is still audible from the dangling headset: "RESCUE DRONES DISPACHED. DO NOT LEAVE YOUR CURRENT POSITION. PURSUIT AUTHORISED."

Is such an Orwellian nightmare so far away? In the last fifty years or so technology has advanced further than we could have imagined and it has radically changed our relationships with each other and with the earth on which we live. In another fifty or perhaps even twenty years will these relationships even be recognisable? Were I to follow an arrow on a screen would I pause to notice how a mountain ridge sweeps down to the glen and rises slightly before I must turn north and head home? Will I scour the glen for a U-shaped bend in the river that shows me where the bothy lies? Will I even notice the rise and fall of a ridge until it deposits me at the summit? I doubt if any of these things will register as I follow the little glowing arrow on the screen.

Were I to worship the god of GPS I think I would miss these things, a little of the poetry would have gone and the lure of the place would be lessened. Instead I think I'll rely on my own frail judgement; I'll make my mistakes and pay for them too.

At home I looked at an up-to-date map of Glen Feshie and

realised I turned back only minutes from the bothy. The map I had been using, I discovered to my alarm, was last revised in 1984. In that time the Berlin Wall has fallen, the Soviet Union dissolved, and – as I learnt to my cost – whole forests have grown from saplings to mature trees.

One day a rescue team may find my frozen body spreadeagled in the snow, having become hopelessly lost in some cataclysmic blizzard. They may shake their heads at my recklessness in having gone out in such conditions without electronic aid, they may regard me as a foolish old man clinging to the technology of a bygone age, but I know this for sure: they will have to tear my compass from my cold dead hand.

The Man From The Ministry

The helicopter lurches violently as it swings around the end of ridge and meets the wind coming down the glen.

"Good of you to come," the slight man, strapped into the chair opposite, yells over the roar of the engine. He struggles with the zip of his white protective suit for a few seconds until it cooperates and he closes the suit under his chin as tightly as he can.

"As soon as we read your blog, we knew you'd be the man for the job." He grins, replacing his bifocals on his aquiline nose.

I return the smile. "You're welcome."

He proffers me a similar suit to his own and is perplexed when I brush it away.

"I'm sorry," he says, thrusting the suit at me again. "Regulations, you know." He wrinkles his nose in disgust. "And there are *natural* things down there. All manner of contamination could occur."

Reluctantly I climb into the suit. As I look up I notice that the four black-uniformed police at the back of the cabin are suiting up too.

Below us a wide green valley sweeps between the rugged hills. The river cuts a silver ribbon through the grass and, on a bend beside the sparkling water, I see a small stone building with a slate roof and a chimney at one end.

"There." I point to the grey-roofed building. "It looks just the sort of place they'd use."

The Man from the Ministry speaks into the wire microphone beside his mouth. "Target located, begin descent." The engine note changes instantly, and the machine sinks into the valley between the hills.

We touch down and the armed police leap from the helicopter and spread out around us in a well-rehearsed routine.

The official types furiously on his tablet then looks at me quizzically. "Is that one of those places they talk about then, a bothy?"

I begin to rise from my chair but the small man motions for me to wait. "Yes, that's right. I've been there before."

He looks up at me in horror.

"In the days before the regulations, of course, a long time ago."

My white-suited companion smiles and nods, obviously relieved. "Several of our surveillance cameras malfunctioned in this area. Then we lost a scouting droid. Just vanished." He shakes his head in disbelief.

"So, you think they might be in the area?" I scan the hills; the area is vast and could hide any number of rebels.

He nods sagely. "Wandering about, unregulated. Imagine it. What about security? What about health and safety? What about insurance?"

I shake my head slowly. "Anything could happen."

In answer he rolls his eyes to the heavens.

"It needs controlling." He pauses, seeking a more appropriate word. "Regulating," he explodes in triumph.

I lean forward and whisper conspiratorially against the roar of the chopper engine. "*Stamping out.*"

He nods again. "Quite right. We can't have this sort of thing, you know."

There is a yell from one of the police officers. "Perimeter secure."

The Man from the Ministry hesitates outside the door of the low stone building. He fiddles with his tablet for a moment, runs his fingers around the elastic collar of his white suit. Finally, he turns to me. "You see, the thing is, there are no procedures for this. It's terribly irregular. Do you think…"

"Of course, not a problem."

He steps aside with evident relief and I draw back the heavy iron bolt on the door. We enter the gloomy interior of this rough stone shelter. As my eyes adjust to the darkness I make out a familiar scene: a wood-lined room, a few rough chairs, a table and an ash-filled fireplace.

I turn to my companion. "They've been here all right."

He types furiously on his tablet. I place my hand on the ashes of the fire. They are cool but not cold.

"Last night I'd say," I declare, taking a pinch of ash and holding it to my nose. I know the smell at once.

I offer the sooty fingertips to the Man from the Ministry, who shrinks back in horror.

"Do you know what that is?" I ask.

"Ash?"

"Ah yes but what kind?"

He shakes his head, mystified.

"This is tobacco ash," I announce.

He stumbles two steps back towards the door. "Tobacco!"

"Pipe tobacco!" I take another sniff and this time I am certain. "It's a special brand. Bothy Bumbler's Twist. And look here." I bend and examine the fire ash carefully, closely watched by the bearer of the tablet. "Whoever knocked out this pipe was left handed."

"You mean they've been smoking in here?" he asks incredulously.

"Oh yes, and drinking too." I hold up an empty can of beer from the corner of the hearth.

"But smoking has been outlawed everywhere. No one is allowed to smoke apart from prisoners on death row. Don't they know the dangers?" He types on his pad for a while until he finally looks up. "Why would they drink alcohol – why don't they drink sterilised water like everyone else?"

I shake my head sadly.

Incensed, the Man from the Ministry begins to hunt around the bothy. He stoops and then holds up some packing in his gloved hand.

He sniffs the wrapping paper. "Sausages!" The veins in his neck are bulging. "For pity's sake they've been eating sausages! Have they no sense? I've eaten only lavender-flavoured couscous for the past ten years!" Now his eyes are standing out of their sockets and sweat is beading on his forehead. "Can you find them?" he demands, his voice almost cracking with panic.

"It won't be easy." I let my eyes wander, looking for more clues, but the bothy is bare. "The Ministry must understand these are desperate men. They cling to a way of life that has been ruled politically incorrect and against the laws of health and safety. These men are forced to lurk in the farthest remote corners of the kingdom where they can enjoy their vile pleasures beyond the reach of the Ministry."

Now the Man from the Ministry is chewing the corner of his tablet. He looks up and fixes me with a steely stare. "You must find them, blogger. The nation is counting on you. Do you know who they are?"

"Yes, I'm afraid I do. These… these men are the Kearvaig Pipe Club."

"There's a club of them?"

"Yes, they travel to remote places, smoke pipes, drink beer and tell each other stories. They even have ceremonial dress: blue dungarees."

"You don't mean," stammers the Man from the Ministry, unable to form the words, "they actually… *enjoy* themselves?"

"I'm afraid so."

"But that was outlawed years ago under the government's *You Can't Be Too Careful* initiative. It's worse than I thought." He grabs the back of a chair to steady himself. "Sausages," he mutters, as if fondly recalling a time long past. "I remember sausages. They used to sizzle so." Overcome, he announces: "I'll need to use the bathroom, do you know where it is?"

I hand him a spade. He looks puzzled for a moment and then the colour drains from his face.

The Man from the Ministry stabs the air with his thin bony fingers, recovering his composure. "They must be stopped."

"I can do it, but you'll have to leave me here for a few days. I need to conduct a thorough search."

He argues, of course, points out the dangers of being alone in such a remote place; but in the end, he sees sense and heads back to the chopper. Four days should do it.

I turn towards the fireplace and examine the wall above it carefully. There is a candle holder fixed to the wood-lined wall. I count the boards to the left; one, two, three. The fourth board is loose. A moment's work and it is free. Behind it is a handle, and when I turn it a door in the wall slides open and a few wisps of pipe smoke drift into the room.

A moment later a tall bald man in blue dungarees steps through the door. Silently he hands me a lit pipe and a glass of whisky. We stand for a moment by the window watching the Man from the Ministry climb into the helicopter. I take a couple of pulls on the pipe and savour the whisky.

The man in dungarees speaks. "What the hell is couscous?"

Folk Lost On The Hill

The large black Labrador shuffled uncomfortably in front of the fire. He was, as is typical of his kind, an expert human watcher and his eyes had strayed little from the angular frame of his owner, who had wedged himself in an armchair for the last hour or so.

Bob could see that his master, *He who wields the tin opener*, was unsettled. For one thing, the TV programme about baking cakes had just finished and he was still awake; for another, every fifteen minutes he would rise up, peer at the clock and sink back into his armchair scratching at the large bush that grew on his chin. Something, Bob decided, was amiss – and he would not settle until George did.

The TV programme about people falling over and being laughed at was halfway through when the phone in the hall rang. *She who provides the odd secret biscuit and is allowed to sleep beside George called through from the Palace of Food*: "I'll get that."

George raised himself half out of the armchair and listened intently. Bob decided that there was definitely something going on, and raised his head from the carpet, focusing his ears on the conversation in the hallway.

"Yes, yes," said the woman George called *darling*, "I see. Oh dear, I'll tell him."

"What is it?" George enquired casually.

"Two more lost on the mountain," Margaret said, wringing her hands in frustration. "I can't believe it, terrible, terrible."

George scratched the remains of his old Aran pullover and rose reluctantly from his armchair. "What can you do?" he muttered, heading for the bedroom and his hill gear.

"I'll make you up some sandwiches, George. I do hope you're not out all night."

A few minutes later George appeared, transformed from the dozing householder to a man of action – well, that might be a slight exaggeration, but he had at least changed his trousers.

"And we were just settling down for a quiet night in. I don't understand it." Margaret emerged from the kitchen with a Tupperware box containing George's carefully wrapped sandwiches. "How many is it now, losing themselves this year?"

George paused in zipping up his fleece. "Oh I don't know, certainly the team's busiest season for years."

"You'd think with GPS and everything there'd be fewer folk getting lost these days."

"Ah well," George mused, shouldering his rucksack, "you know these hills – the weather can change terrible quick, folk just get caught out."

Margaret proffered the box of sandwiches. "I've made them from that nice low-fat cheese and the cholesterol-reducing spread instead of butter. Oh and there's that reduced-fat mayonnaise you like too. Your favourite."

George smiled and, leaning forward to peck Margaret on the cheek, reflected on how middle age had seeped into every corner of his life; now even his sandwiches reeked more of medical advice than taste. The days of bacon sandwiches and white bread soaked in tomato sauce had long gone, along with his flowing hair.

* * *

The car park at the foot of the glen was already busy with team members and abandoned cars by the time George steered his Volvo to a halt beside the white-and-red Land Rover, the team's proud possession. Jumble sales and sponsored walks over a number of years had raised enough cash to fund the vehicle. Each tyre was the product of the sale of threadbare trousers and many miles of soggy walking by willing volunteers.

Kenny was lounging from the driver's window, his woollen hat in danger of losing the fight to contain his mop of curly ginger hair. He waved to George as he stepped from his car.

"Well here we are again." His soft voice was almost lost against the burbling of a nearby burn.

"Aye, here we are again," replied George as he fastened his boots.

"Search the bothy first I thought?" Kenny heaved the long aluminium silhouette of the stretcher from the back of the team vehicle. "Charlie and the rest of the boys have gone ahead."

"Not all boys," George said, noticing Constable Laura's patrol car parked a few feet away. Laura was always first at any rescue and her stamina was a legend amongst the team.

Kenny smiled. "Ah well no that's true. They'll do well to keep up with her."

The last of the evening light was slipping quietly from the

glen and the November air was already turning chill as the two men (and one dog) headed up into the hills along the path beside the burn. They walked in silence, wheeling the stretcher with its load of chinking equipment between them. The track climbed steeply at first and the ascent demanded all the breath both men had before it gradually eased a mile or so before the bridge across the gorge. It was here the two allowed themselves a pause. It was fully dark now and they both stood for a moment, watching their breath mist in the beams from their head torches.

George looked up and noticed that the stars were already beginning to show as pinpricks in the night sky. "A frost tonight, I think. I take it we are well equipped for whatever rigours we may face?"

Kenny sounded offended. "You don't think I'd leave us short?"

In a mile, the bothy came into view, a dull glow emanating from the windows. A tall, slim female figure was first to greet them from the door.

"What kept you?"

George was all business. "Have you located the casualties, Laura?"

Laura's quick hands pushed her hair back from her face and revealed her piercing eyes. She shot George a look as though he had asked if midges bite. "Of course we have – here they are."

Inside the bothy, candles flickered and a small fire was struggling to keep the night air at bay. A middle-aged couple were seated on a rickety bench, both nursing cups of steaming tea.

George hurried over to them. "I can't thank you enough," he

declared.

"Oh you're very welcome," the couple replied in unison. "Any time."

"I don't think we'd be wise to descend tonight," Kenny mused aloud, calling from the darkness beyond the bothy door.

George followed the voice and found Kenny, Laura and half a dozen team members staring into the darkness to the glen below. By now the valley was bathed in moonlight with the folds of the low hills showing black against the starlit backdrop. Already, tiny ice crystals were sparkling on the heather. All eyes turned expectantly to George; as leader, it would be his call.

"Well…" George looked at the sky, smelt the wind, touched the cold night air with his fingers. "It's all right now, isn't it? We could set off and it could be fine." There was a murmur of concerned assent. "But," George pronounced the words as though he were a judge sentencing a murderer to death, "It could all change in an instant. You can never tell."

"No, no, in an instant… never tell." The company echoed George's words with dire solemnity.

"I think it wise to stay here for the night."

En masse the team turned and rushed for the bothy door and, after a moment of jostling, all were inside.

Kenny began to unwrap the load on the stretcher. "Best unpack the equipment," he said with some relish.

The following emerged from the folds: two fiddles, one harmonica (bent), four bottles assorted malt whisky, six packs of lager and four of beer, two wine boxes, several packs of sausages, bacon, eggs, cheese, one pack of cards, a large bag of coal and – to the surprise of nearly everyone – a bottle of vodka.

Laura picked up the bottle of clear liquid and examined it appreciatively. "Well now. Not everyone drinks whisky." She spoke in a clear, crisp tone that she used to reprimand the village drunks when they misbehaved on Saturday nights; no one argued.

* * *

Some time later George sat cradling a glass of his favourite and staring into the bothy fire. Bob lay upside down warming his stomach before the flames.

"I feel a little hungry," he remarked, mainly to himself as his words were lost amongst the babble of voices and the whine of the fiddle.

He popped open the little plastic box and carefully unwrapped the delicately prepared sandwiches. He took a moment to enjoy the aroma of cheese and mayonnaise, noticing how the lettuce hung forlornly between the layers of gluten-free bread. Then, with a deft flick of the wrist, he hurled them into the bothy fire where they lay sizzling for a moment before the flames consumed them.

"How're those sausages coming along, Kenny?" he called.

At the word 'sausages' Bob awoke from his slumbers by the bothy fire and wagged his tail.

George bent down and rubbed Bob behind the ear. "Don't worry, you'll get yours. It's a good job, isn't it, that every now and again folk get lost on the hill."

Bob didn't hear that; his mind was focused on the frying pan.

This story has been published on tgomagazine.co.uk (The Great Outdoors).

The Ghost Bothy

As I step off the bus on the ski road, an icy blast hits and sends me scuttling into my pack for my cagoule and balaclava. Safely ensconced beneath itchy wool and armoured by my orange nylon cagoule I can take a few moments to scan this alien horizon. The Northern Corries of the Cairngorms rise above me, a vast landscape of ice-wreathed cliffs, the white glaze broken here and there by dark ridges of rock: a scene drained of colour, painted only in black and white. A thousand feet below, a green ring of forest surrounds the outline of Loch Morlich, its waters frozen and still. I have spent weekends in the snowy Lake District, even visited Glen Coe in the winter, but these are the Cairngorms – a place wracked by ferocious winds and merciless blizzards. I am about to step into a different league.

I had a week's 'study leave' from my social work course in Leicester. If you say 'study leave' to a climber it means only one thing, 'time to go climbing'. I originally planned to go climbing in the accessible corries of the Northern Cairngorms with a fellow student but, at the last moment, he had remembered something he urgently needed to do. I suspect he'd remembered that he wanted to stay alive. So here I am heading off into the vast snowy wastes of the Cairngorms alone.

This is Easter in the Highlands. Easter in Britain's mountains, even in the 1970s, is the ficklest of seasons. Easter can be deepest winter or early summer; there is no telling which. This Easter, to my delight, Britain has been hit by an Arctic blast and the hills are covered with deep drifts of snow. The weather in the Cairngorms is, as ever, more savage than most.

As I emerge from the tree line, the east wind begins to tug at my clothing and sends snowflakes battering into my face. Below and to my right, the outline of Loch Morlich is etched by trees even though its waters have long ago succumbed to the ice and drifting snow. To my left loom the cliffs of Coire an Lochain and Coire an t-Sneachda. I am at once overwhelmed by the sheer scale of the place – this is a mountain environment far grander in its sweeping cliffs and open corries than anything I have seen before. My goal this day is the Sinclair Memorial Hut. I know nothing of this place other than it is marked on the map as a small square on the side of the great glen that cuts through the Cairngorms, the Lairig Ghru. I am cautious of this pass. Its reputation is fearsome and I am gingerly approaching the edges of the mountain king's domain.

The path climbs below the northern corries to a point where the way to the Lairig Ghru is barred by a big ridge that descends all the way from the Cairngorm Plateau itself. This ridge has one weakness, the Chalamain Gap – a jagged slash, like a sword cut – that slices through the ridge. As I arrive, the blizzard is accelerating and I am grateful at first for the shelter of the gap. I say at first because soon the hidden dangers of the gap reveal themselves. The floor is littered with a jumble of huge boulders, and fresh snow has covered the leg-breaking gaps between the rocks. A slip here, with a heavy pack, could have serious consequences. It takes me an age to pick my way between the mantraps until I am finally able to descend into the Lairig Ghru. Once down in this huge glen I look up and there, perched above me, is the outline of the small bothy.

* * *

"Ere, lad, grab this."

Almost before I can sit down a hand thrusts a steaming mug of tea towards me. I'm sitting in a concrete box filled with steam and three or four sweating bodies. It's dark inside and I can barely make out the silhouettes of the other occupants of this tomb-like dwelling. One of them is struggling with an ancient Primus stove on the floor while the other two mock his efforts.

"You'se can sleep over there," he says amicably.

Before I can respond one of his companions butts in: "Tell him to fuck off. He's always organising people."

It transpires that these are climbers from Cumbria come to climb the Angel's Ridge. They call the crouching figure 'El Presidente' as he is their club president. They argue amiably between themselves and greet me, their young, inexperienced companion, with a gruff benevolence. They seem old to me – they might be forty – but their experience is vast compared to mine and I sit in awe of them. This is my first meeting with 'The Brotherhood', and I feel as if I have entered a hidden world occupied by men of a different race.

We are only a few miles from the Highland town of Aviemore, with its shops, pubs and streetlights, yet high on that hill, as darkness descends, it feels as though the mundane world has drifted off into a different universe. Our world shrinks to the confines of these four concrete walls, lit by candles and heated only by our bodies. The three climbers, happy to include me in their company, swap tales about their adventures.

"We were on't Isle o Man," a stocky man tells me, sporting a flat cap and smoking an acrid pipe. "I was climbing this sea cliff. It were like climbing a pile o' crisps. Every 'old was crumbing away, it were desperate. I were near the top when this posh bloke sticks 'is head over the edge and starts telling me how I shouldn't be climbing there. I told 'im I knew I shouldn't be there and I said if I got off the crag alive I'd throw him down the bloody thing."

His mates had probably heard this tale a hundred times but it doesn't stop them greeting its climax with raucous laughter.

I listen avidly to their tales of adventures on wild Lakeland fells, hear their stories of savage winter storms and nights in distant bothies. Adversity makes real tales but, like a failed love affair, it is something best admired from a distance. As I close my eyes that night, warm in my sleeping bag, I drift into the land of dreams wondering if one day I'd have stories of my own to tell.

The next day we set off early, heading into the vast frozen heart of the Cairngorm mountains. I know I am out of my depth, alone in severe conditions, and when I discover this band of ancient warriors would be heading part of the way to my goal of Corrour bothy I ask if I can join them. Fresh snow fell overnight and we sink to our thighs as we struggle through the great V-shaped chasm that is the Lairig Ghru. I am overwhelmed by the scale of this place. On either side huge white slopes head up into the clouds, their summits lost to the inexorable whiteness. I am used to the scale of the Lake District, where you are never that far from a farm, a village or a friendly pub. That is not the case here, I realise – in these mountains it feels as though you could wander endlessly through an arctic landscape and never escape. There are no dry-stone walls here; in fact there seems little sign of man's hand at all.

We trudge through the deep snow in silence, each of us muffled beneath woolly hats and nylon hoods, content to listen to the rhythm of our breathing. The high point of the pass is where our routes diverge. We shake hands and they head off towards the great cliffs of Coire Etchachan. I watch as their figures are slowly swallowed by the falling snow. I am alone and vulnerable again.

The falling snow thickens and now all I can see is a wall of white. I worry that I will miss the bothy and head off into the nothingness beyond. The going is slow, and I struggle to follow what little I can see of the path. Here there are no waymarkers, nothing but the featureless white. This is a world I have never experienced before – it is far greater in scale than my familiar Cumbria. I am walking in a featureless world.

My eyes strain into the whiteness, searching for a sign of the bridge that leads to the bothy. As I peer into the snow, my face is bombarded by snowflakes that tickle my skin and eyelashes. There is a river to my right that I glimpse fleetingly through the blizzard. These are the only two things I know for certain: somewhere in the whiteness there is the bothy, and a bridge across the river, but I don't know where.

I have lost track of time. I might have been walking for

an hour or possibly two. In the white wasteland distance is impossible to gauge and I am growing increasingly concerned by my isolation, alone in the great white nothing. A shape appears before me – suddenly there is something black in all this whiteness. It is an iron post about a metre high, a sudden reassurance that a human world exists somewhere beyond the white. Looking down I see footprints in the snow and realise that this post is a waymarker. The footprints lead towards the river and soon I find myself clattering over a little metal bridge, the steel unfamiliar beneath my boots, the water cold and grey below. Then there is the muffled sound of voices, their resonance subdued by the snow-filled air.

The small stone-built shelter emerges from the snowstorm. It has only one door and one window, its roof is buried by the snow, and icicles hang from its gutters. At that moment it feels as if I have arrived at the loneliest place on Earth.

It's dark in the bothy and I am glad to rest my eyes from the unending white. The building has stone walls, dank with condensation, and the floor is earth, compacted hard by countless feet. There is a fireplace but it is dead, dark and cold. There is nothing to burn here and no one can carry fuel this far in these conditions.

A young woman greets me. Her hair is dark, and I can only make out her eyes and the flash of her teeth in her smile in the gloom. "Welcome to the Ritz. I'll call the porter to take your bags."

I laugh and my breath mists in the cold air.

"It's a good job you weren't here last night," she adds, "I don't know where we'd have put you – the place was heaving with folk."

"Where can I sleep?" I cast my eyes around the tiny bothy, looking for a corner to spread out my mat.

The young woman shivers and pulls the zip of her fibre-pile jacket up to her chin. "The four-poster is occupied, but you can have over here." She points to a section of earth covered by the orange plastic of old survival bags.

A handful of young men are squatting on the floor around gas stoves or huddled in sleeping bags. It is like a scene from the 15th century – there is so little to show that the modern world exists. It's so cold that the only place to be is in my sleeping bag. Soon everyone else is dozing. In the 15th century, when it goes dark, you go to bed.

I'm woken by a sudden commotion in the darkness. Torches flash around the bothy as two men stagger through the door. They are barely coherent and mutter about being lost for hours and wading through the river. The bothy bursts into life and soon mugs of tea are being thrust into trembling fingers. I spend half an hour cracking the ice off one man's gaiters so he can get his boots off and find some dry socks. As I snuggle back into my sleeping bag, their entrance brings home to me that the Cairngorms are an unforgiving place.

I wake the next morning to grey skies in this still-frozen waste. I plan to stay here another night. In our chatter, it emerges that the young woman I spoke to when I arrived is leaving, along with everyone else. I set off to climb the Devil's Point (Bod an Deamhain), a pointed hill that rises directly behind the bothy. As I climb the weather deteriorates and visibility – poor at the outset – closes in to a mere fifty feet or so. I reach the ridge above the bothy and the wind rises, jostling me about like a subway crowd. I am at the edge of my confidence. I realise that if I head up the peak and then miss the small gap in the ridge that leads to the descent I might never get back to the little shelter and, without those four stone walls, survival would be a grim battle. I give in to the gremlins battling in my stomach and return to Corrour, which now stands empty.

I crawl into my sleeping bag and pass the afternoon reading the novel *Papillon* by Henri Charrière while the wind rages outside. The novel covers the trials of a man desperate to escape imprisonment. The hero's struggles and privations make the hardships I am enduring seem mild.

That night something happens. So far in my Cairngorm odyssey the only sound has been the wind, but now there is another sound: I can hear water dripping. I open the bothy door and something remarkable has happened. It is pouring with rain. In a matter of hours, the Ice Queen has leapt upon her sleigh and ridden off into the distance. Winter is over. The next day most of the snow has gone and the transformation is almost complete as bare earth emerges everywhere.

Unfortunately, earth is not the only thing that emerges. There are no toilets in this bothy in the 1970s, and over the past few snowy weeks guests have relieved themselves in a circle with a radius of about a hundred yards from the bothy. I am surrounded by an almost perfect faecal fairy ring. I decide it is time to go.

Glen Tilt is a long, long glen. I have been walking for hours, my boots are full of water and my feet hurt. I am forced to wade stream after stream as they swell with meltwater and overwelm the paths beside them. The landscape is unrecognisable from yesterday: heathery hillsides and little stone walls, babbling burns, patches of snow shrinking before my eyes.

I am aiming for the Highland village of Blair Atholl, hoping against hope I can get there before the pub shuts. At 9.00 p.m., after walking around 27 miles, I am forced to concede that this is beyond my reach with only five miles to go. Too tired to erect my tent, I put on my duvet jacket, hastily erect a small bivouac in the trees and fall into an exhausted sleep.

It's about 03.00 a.m. when I wake, cold, damp and shivering. The heavy dew has soaked through my gear and it is now obvious that I need my tent. Half asleep, I put it up, crawl into my sleeping bag and am soon snoring in luxurious warmth.

I wake in the forest: a soft moss carpet beneath me, the scent of pine trees filling the air. A mist fills the steep-sided glen and wraiths the trees. I have no food left now so, after a breakfast of black tea, I head for the fleshpots of Blair Atholl.

* * *

The woman in the post office watches me suspiciously as I browse the rack of postcards. I catch sight of my reflection in the shop window and instantly understand why. Four days of wandering through the Cairngorm winter have taken their toll. The woollen RAF trousers my uncle gave me are now battered and stained. My grimy face boasts a few days' stubble. In the hills none of that mattered, but down here, amongst the pristine white envelopes, I look distinctly disreputable.

She emerges from behind the counter, and her expression suggests she is convinced I am a tramp, about to make off with a huge supply of postcards stuffed down my trousers.

"Can I help you?" she asks, wringing her hands like a Church of Scotland minister addressing a sinner.

As I step out of the shop doorway and lift my rucksack onto my shoulders, a police car draws up beside me. It's a Morris Minor, built more for comfort than speed. Two officers regard me with suspicion through the windscreen. As I turn to leave they both get out of the car and head my way.

"Have you got a moment, sir?" the older of the two asks me. He is stout and squeezed in to his uniform, and his tone makes it clear that a negative answer is not an option.

The police station is warm and dry, and I am happy enough to be there. I am in a place with heating, electric light and running water; after living in the 15th century for the last few days it is impossibly luxurious.

The detective is a stout man in his fifties with a moustache reeking of stale cigarette smoke. "So, where have you been?"

"I've just walked through the Lairig Ghru," I explain cheerfully.

The detective looks at me quizzically. He's obviously never walked up a hill in his life and has no idea what I just said. "That's an unusual route, isn't it?" he says, perhaps in the hope of shaking my story.

Since I haven't done anything wrong, I'm completely relaxed. "It's probably the best-known route in the Cairngorms."

He looks unconvinced. "What's in this bag, then?"

"There's a tent and sleeping bag and a stove. And I've got a head torch. It fits onto my head."

He seems very interested in my light. This is the late 70s and head torches are only known to the mountaineering and caving fraternities.

"So I can climb in the dark, you see," I add.

He toys with the end of his moustache, deep in thought. "Did anyone see you who can vouch for you in this Larry Grew?"

The girl I spoke to in Corrour, the Cumbrian climbers and anyone else who may have seen me have dispersed into the ether. I have no idea how to contact them.

In the end he settles for my cover story, that of being a social work student on study leave. "Who can we call to confirm you are who you say you are?"

This is tricky – I'm supposed to be studying after all. In the end I get them to phone the college, who confirm I am who I say I am. Quite how I am going to explain my week's study leave being spent in Cairngorm blizzards I'm not too sure. After an hour or so they release me.

I turn to the detective on the steps of the police station. "What did you think I'd done?"

"Oh," he says, lighting a cigarette, "we thought you were a cat burglar."

Perhaps telling them about my head torch wasn't such a good idea.

* * *

When I went back to my social work course, my tutor never said a word about my week's study leave in the Cairngorms. They knew me better than I thought; my fondness for wild places was obvious, and it was exactly what they expected me to do.

The icy shelter of Corrour bothy, with its primitive stone walls and medieval feel, left its mark on me. I found myself raving about the place to friends who had never been there, struggling to describe the sheer scale and remoteness of the great glen of the Lairig Ghru itself. In my dreams I walked through those snows once more.

* * *

The following winter, I began my first tentative steps into winter climbing with some easy gullies in the Lake District and Glen Coe. Now the romance of the Angel's Ridge called to me. The thought that I might be able to follow the adventures of the Cumbrian climbers I had met amidst the snows that Easter was a torment.

Almost a year later, during an icy February, I am once again searching through the Cairngorm snows for that small stone refuge. The wind howls down the glen as darkness begins to descend, driving the blizzard into my face with ever-increasing vigour.

"There's a post somewhere," I cry, struggling to make myself heard over the wind.

Charles waits behind me, reluctant to emerge from the shelter of my body and brave the full force of the wind. We are an incongruous pair. He is a barrister, the product of a public-school education, who speaks with a cut-glass upper-class accent. I am the product of the secondary modern school's system and decidedly rough around the edges. But class, status and occupation are all meaningless in the mountains. He and I enjoy each other's company and, in my mind, his sense of humour more than makes up for the disability of his class.

"I say, do you think it's much further?" he says, like Bertie

Wooster asking Jeeves about the proximity of the nearest eatery.

I scan the vast whiteness before me for the little post I had seen three years earlier – the post that had shown me the route to the bridge leading to Corrour. It's almost dark now. My feeble head-torch beam dwindles away into the worst blizzard I've ever experienced. Charles and I are approaching the bothy from the south this time; my first visit was from the north. The walk in from the Linn of Dee looked simple enough on the map, and on a sunny day it probably is – but in the dark night of a Cairngorm blizzard it was proving anything but simple.

Charles had insisted that we call in at the cosy little cafe in Ballater where he consumed a huge steaming plate of haggis, neeps and tatties while I watched the fingers of the clock, anxious to make the bothy before nightfall.

"Got to feed the inner man, old bean," he had replied when I protested about the delay.

Now, with the cafe many miles behind us, his craving for the Scottish delicacy is costing us dear. In the thigh-deep snow I have no idea where the path is. We've been walking a long time in the blizzard and I am growing concerned that we have passed the post and are carrying on to the vast emptiness beyond the remote shelter.

"I think we'd better put the tent up," I suggest to Charles, ice crystals freezing against my eyelashes as I peer into the snows.

The flimsy green nylon shelter bucks in the increasing wind and I climb fully dressed into my prize passion, a Canadian down sleeping bag that I purchased on my very first credit card. I'm going to be paying off that debt for a long time, but tonight, in the middle of an icy Cairngorm blizzard, the investment seems justified. I find myself warm and comfortable despite the conditions. Charles is less lucky: his sleeping bag is a poor affair and I can feel him shivering against my back in the cramped confines of the tent. As I begin to drift off to sleep I decide that I'll spend a couple of hours in my bag and then give it to Charles for an hour or so to prevent him dying of exposure. This is a sincerely held intention.

I close my eyes for a moment and when I open them bright sunlight is streaming into the tent. Something odd has happened: I can't move my legs. Overnight, snow has blown underneath the flysheet and built up in a huge internal cornice. I feel guilty that I spent a night in luxury while Charles slept fitfully in the bitter cold of an inadequate sleeping bag. Anyone who has spent an interminable night out in the cold will know the aching tedium that such an experience brings as you feel every second of darkness tick by.

I wriggle out of the tent and am blinded for a moment by the intense sunlight. I can barely believe that just a few hours ago the glen was wracked by a blizzard. Now the air is still and the steep-sided valley sparkles in reflected sunlight. Then I notice, not ten feet from the tent, the post I passed three years ago. Corrour bothy is only a hundred yards away.

Charles stirs reluctantly, warm for the first time in hours. "I think I'll pop off home today."

I'm dismayed. "But the weather's amazing now."

Despite my pleas, Charles is in no mood to spend another night freezing in his inadequate sleeping bag, and sets off to trudge back to the Linn of Dee and hitch-hike back to Sheffield.

* * *

The bothy has changed little in the few years since I was here. Last night, according to the bothy logbook, there were ten folk squeezed into every inch of the earth floor. Now my disgruntled climbing partner has departed for warmer climes any possibility of an Angel's Ridge ascent has departed with him.

This time I make it to the summit of the Devil's Point, and the whole of the Cairngorms spreads out before me. From the summit I gaze out across a rolling sea of white peaks with no mark of the hand of man apart from the little bothy huddled at the foot of the cliffs. The sky seems bigger here – it is deep blue, and a few pristine white clouds drift gently across the endless void.

I stand for a long time on the summit of this remote peak. Part of me is trying to gain some rational understanding of the distances I am perceiving, but I am half conscious of another process within me. It is as if just as I look at the landscape it too sees me. The young man in a cagoule, with a woollen hat and an ice axe, is also part of the landscape.

* * *

A lot changes in forty years. You get jobs, get married and have kids – well, maybe kids have you is the truth of it. Forty years have passed since a young social work student fought his way through a blizzard and on to Corrour. It is that long since I trod the snows of the Lairig Ghru and spent the night sleeping on the hard earth of the crowded bothy.

Now, as my boots crunch into the hard-packed snow, I am heading up the V-shaped valley of the Lairig Ghru once more.

I can hardly believe I am here once more after all these years. It is the Tuesday after Easter, almost exactly the same time of year as my previous visit. This time I have a plan: I intend to spend the night in Corrour and then walk out over the vast, white whalebacks of the mountains until finally I can stride over the summit of Braeriach and descend once more into the great valley and return to my car.

That walk feels a long way off now and I am by no means certain I'll have the fitness or the right conditions to complete the walk. I half expect that all I will do is spend the night in the bothy and then retrace my steps in the morning. The first objective is the bothy – and that seems enough of a challenge as I contemplate the miles of snow-covered country that lie between me and that tiny shelter. The years that have passed have changed me more than the landscape. The slim, long-haired twenty-year-old has been replaced by a bald, thick-waisted middle-aged man.

But the landscape has changed a little as well. The bothy where I met the Cumbrian climbers, and shared their tea and yarns, was demolished in 1991. To give it its full name, the Angus Sinclair Memorial Hut was built in 1957 as a memorial to an officer in the Officer Training Corps who died during a training exercise a few years before. It had always been a spartan place, even by bothy standards: a box built of breeze blocks with one window and a flat roof. In cold weather – and isn't it always cold at 2,000 feet in the Cairngorms? – condensation ran down the walls and formed in pools on the floor, which was covered with a sort of wooden decking to keep the inhabitants away from the waterlogged concrete. Over the years many exhausted hill-goers must have found sanctuary within its walls, drunk tea and whisky and swapped tall tales and lies in a dank world, filled with steam and the hissing of old Primus stoves whilst outside the storm raged.

I returned to the Sinclair hut, known to devotees as 'The Sinky', only once and that was during my time with the Cairngorm Mountain Rescue Team. A hillwalker had been taken ill whilst out walking and he and his companions had taken refuge in the little shelter whilst a couple of folk had hurried down to the ski tow on Cairngorm to raise the alarm. I think it was about 1.00 a.m. by the time the team reached the hut. In my memory there was a blizzard but I'm not sure if the blizzard was real or is just a trick of the mind. Most of the rescues I can recall took place in wild snowstorms but I can't help wondering if I'm mentally transposing those storms onto every rescue I took part in.

It was dark, I am certain of that, and I and the other members of the team milled around outside the hut whilst the doctor examined the stricken walker. It was decided that it would be best to evacuate the man – who had by now been elevated to the status of casualty – and get him to hospital in Inverness as quickly as possible.

If you have never carried another human being any distance on a stretcher, let me enlighten you as to how much of an ordeal it is for all concerned, including the occupant of the stretcher. For the next hour and a half this poor walker was swung to and fro, surrounded by a group of sweating, staggering men and women who only paused to issue some obscene expletive when the rocks underfoot managed to rick a knee or turn an ankle. A stretcher is a heavy rectangular thing that doesn't like going in anything other than a straight line and does its very best to hurl the humans carrying it into the nearest abyss. The width of a stretcher means that those on either side carrying it are always walking off the edge of all but the widest of paths. So you stumble and fall most of the way. The terrain is never level so the folk on one side of a stretcher are always trying to get it up or down to their level whilst the people on the other side do the same.

It takes about sixteen folk working in shifts to carry a stretcher a few miles. It's for this reason that we all staggered, dripping with sweat, to the road with our casualty, like James Bond's cocktails, 'shaken but not stirred'.

The walk in to Corrour brings vivid memories of that stretcher carry back to me. I have only carried in a handful of coal; I expect there will be a mob of folk in there this Easter as the weather forecast is so good, and I can just add my coal to theirs. But when at last I push open the bothy door I find the place deserted. This little bothy has changed a great deal since I walked here as a student. Gone is the earth floor, replaced by wood. The stone walls are now lined with wood and there are even toilets to the rear of the building. If you're picturing a white-tiled sanitary palace with flushing loos and electric hand driers, you will be sadly disappointed. They are composting toilets, based on old Chinese principles, that allow human waste to biodegrade and become fertiliser. Crude as they are, they are a massive improvement on folk crapping in the nearest hole in the snow.

From the footprints in the deep snow it's obvious that there were lots of people here only yesterday, Easter Monday. Now, most of those folk are back in the office with only tired legs to remind them of their Cairngorm adventures. The convivial night in front of the bothy fire I had hoped for is not to be; there will be no fire at all as I don't have enough coal to get a blaze going.

As darkness falls on the little bothy the temperature outside falls well below zero and the temperature inside is only a little higher. I pass the night dozing in my sleeping bag. Every time I fall asleep the wind rattles the bothy door like some lost traveller trying to get inside. Eventually I have to wedge the door shut with a chair and can get some peace from nocturnal rattlings.

* * *

I wake early, as soon as the thin light penetrates the bothy window. Glancing up from my sleeping bag I realise it is misty outside. The weather must have broken last night and my heart sinks as I realise that all chance of walking out over the summits has gone. Then I look again at the mist and discover that it's caused not by the weather outside but by condensation inside. A cold wind hits me as I open the bothy door but the sky is clear and bodes well for the coming day. There is no time to lose; I pack away my sleeping bag and brew some tea.

The route I have planned is a serious undertaking, one of the most serious mountain walks in Britain. I'll leave the bothy, climb over the summits of Stob Coire an t-Saighdeir and Cairn Toul, then follow the broad ridge of Sgor an Lochain Uaine (the Angel's Peak) before finally climbing the long gentle ridge of Braeriach. Only then can I descend to the Lairig Ghru once more and back to my waiting car.

The walk is not serious in the sense that there is a danger of falling. What makes it serious is that, once I make the climb up and over Cairn Toul there is no easy way back – I will be in the heart of remote country with a long walk home in any direction. On this walk I could be exposed to the worst weather the arctic plateau has to offer. At its worst, that weather could be a threat to my survival. If I encounter deep, soft snow it will sap my strength and slow me to a crawl, meaning I could be walking well into darkness before I finally make it home.

All this is compounded by the fact that I am, of course, alone. There isn't another human being for miles and, should the weather close in, I'll probably have the whole of the Cairngorms to myself. I am totally reliant on my own resources and at the mercy of the weather and snow conditions. This is not walking – this is winter mountaineering and a serious business. Experienced as I am, I feel more than a little trepidation, or even fear, as my crampons bite into the icy crust of the snowslope leading to the gap in the ridge, which I climbed through as a student all those years ago. I've learned that, in the mountains, fear is your friend; it's fear that keeps you alive. And anyway, in the Cairngorms no one can hear you scream.

I have a theory about life in the mountains. You spend days plodding through lousy weather with no views and water trickling down your back. You do that over and over again through the most miserable conditions and then, and only then, do the mountain gods smile on you. Once you have made that sacrifice they reach down and touch you, and give the gift of a day so perfect that you will remember it for the rest of your life.

This is such a day. As I gain the ridge, the sky clears to a peerless blue, the sun shines, the wind drops to nothing, and the snow is frozen iron hard. It is a day in a thousand and I can barely believe my luck. Nevertheless, the climb from the col to the first summit is a long slog. I am dressed for cold and in these alpine conditions sweat drips from me as I climb. I am still conscious of the time, knowing I have a long way to go. At last I reach the first summit. Across the glen I can see the distant top of Ben MacDui and beyond that Cairn Gorm itself. I can make out the tiny specks of walkers, dwarfed by the landscape, reaching the summit of Ben MacDui. The plateau is eerily silent; no wind dances amongst the ice crystals that sparkle on the surface of the snow. The reflected light is so bright I have to peer through closed eyelids. Apart from the distant people on Ben MacDui I am the only figure in the vast arctic wasteland.

One question haunts me: do I have enough time to complete the walk before darkness? I'm glad that this is late March – I have more hours of daylight than I would in January. Perhaps I could complete the walk in darkness by following my head-torch beam through the mountains but I am already a little intimidated by this enterprise and nightfall would bring other problems I would rather avoid. I am moving very slowly on the ascent of Cairn Toul. It is taking much longer than I had planned and the bright, unexpectedly hot sun makes me sweat. At last I arrive at the summit, blowing hard from the exertion. I wonder if I am fit enough; I still have a long way to go.

The summit of Braeriach sparkles in the morning sun ahead of me, its corries crystal clear. Leaning on my walking poles I can't help but think that I still have a huge amount of distance between me and that summit, the last before I can descend to the valley below. I reassure myself that the snow is hard and I should make reasonable time but my doubts refuse to dissipate. Once I head down from this peak and travel north towards the bealach between this and the next summit I will be committed; it will take the same amount of effort to retreat as it would to continue. I take a deep breath and head for the col below.

Released from the effort of the climb, my speed increases. The snow is in perfect condition for walking, and ice crystals crunch with every step as I run down the graceful arc of the ridge, finding myself at the col within minutes. Here I have a choice: I can climb to the summit of the Angel's Peak or cut across its slopes, saving myself a few minutes and a lot of exertion. I'm still worried about the time factor and I feel alone and vulnerable in this place. The classic line would be to climb to the next summit but I am a long way from home and such esoteric considerations are not high on my list of priorities. I choose the straightforward option of getting home alive.

I decide to save time by traversing the slope and omitting the next climb. The snow is deeper than expected and halfway across the slope I realise that the full sun has been on this area for a long time. Worried about the possibility of avalanche, I unfasten the waist belt of my rucksack, prepared for a quick getaway should the slope betray me. I calculate that the slope is unlikely to develop a large slide, but I might be wrong – and there is no such thing as being caught in a good avalanche.

Safely on the next col, out of danger, I fasten my rucksack straps again and breathe more easily. Below me the great icy bowl of Garbh Choire Mor stretches to the Lairig Ghru, which I had walked through only yesterday to the bothy. Soon I am making rapid progress and the summit of Braeriach, which seemed so far away only hours ago, is looming closer with every step. I begin to relax and enjoy the rhythm of moving through this ancient landscape.

Above the glens, the summits of the Cairngorms are much as they were thousands of years ago; little has changed here since the last ice age. I am at peace now, no longer concerned about the possibility of a long exhausting march. The snow conditions are perfect and I am confident I can complete the walk. I listen to the rhythm of my breath, to my boots crunching the ice, to my walking poles' reassuring impact on the snow. There is a perfect simplicity to these movements, a natural harmony with the landscape. My body sings with joy.

At the summit of Braeriach the ridge narrows to only a few feet wide. Looking back I notice a figure, perhaps half a mile away, walking on the plateau. He or she must have come up from the north and is the first human being I've seen close at hand for two days. The figure is dwarfed by the cliffs of Garbh Choire Mor, tiny and inconsequential against their enormity. You could drop Saint Paul's Cathedral into these mountain bowls and lose it.

* * *

On the drive home to Inverness, my legs aching, I feel relaxed and complete. I realise that I may never experience such a day again. So many things had to come together for me to complete that walk successfully, for it to be as perfect as it had been. I had to be free at the right moment, fit enough, and the weather and snow conditions had to be just right. All these factors my never combine again in my lifetime. I have been given a gift by the mountain gods, and it is something I will treasure.

~

The Journey Continues

If you have enjoyed this book please take a moment to place a review on Amazon.

To learn more about some of the characters and places that appear in this book visit John D Burns website where you'll find photos, podcasts and blogs about John's adventures in the hills.

You can also download the first two chapters of his first book, *The Last Hillwalker*, free to your e-reader, from John's website:

johndburns.com

Also By John D Burns

The Last Hillwalker

A sideways look at forty years in Britain's mountains

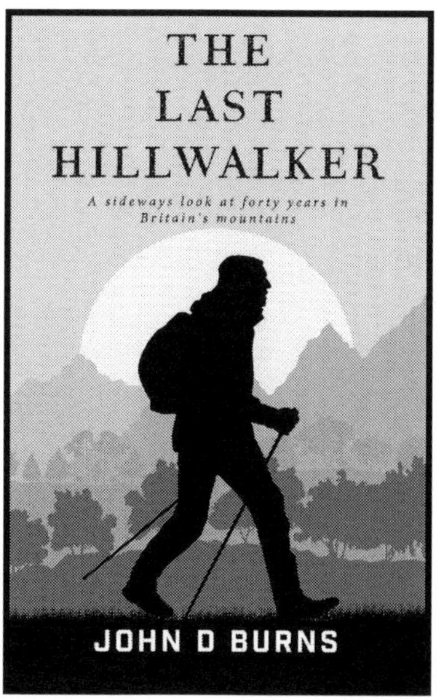

Captures the essence of what it means to love mountains and love being in mountains.

Chris Townsend, The Great Outdoors Magazine

A compulsively readable book that, with insight and humour, takes the reader through a life's journey on the hills and mountains. Well structured, starting with a white-knuckle epic on an icebound Ben Nevis to very effectively hook the reader in, leading into a well-organised read.

Neil Reid, Mountaineering Scotland

This is one of the best books I have read this year. Breathtaking accounts of mountaineering and rock climbing with a brilliant sense of humour. The descriptions are amazing and you experience the pain, fear, danger and jubilation with the author.

Amazon Review

The most compelling thing about these tales is that they are 'our tales', the tales of mountain lovers. If you've ever enjoyed the 'pleasures' of being cold and wet on a mountain, being lost in a blizzard, or any of the other daft things that climbers and mountaineers do, you will enjoy this book. It tells our story, the stories of mountain folk.

Paul Sharrock, Blogger

Visit johndburns.com to download the first two chapters free to your e-reader.

The Last Hillwalker

An Extract

My mind races to a scene in the future. I'm in the Old Dungeon Ghyll, it's December, and outside the snow is falling thick and fast. Inside I'm sitting by the glowing fire, pint of Old Peculier in hand, relating my tale of how we rescued a Frenchman from certain death in the Alps. Amongst climbers such tales – or epics, are they are known – are the food and drink of pub evenings. Such stories form the legends and folk tales that bind together this small group of outsiders. Doubtless I will exaggerate a little, perhaps even lie; but none of that matters. It's the tale that is told that counts.

Twenty thousand years ago men hunched around fires, pinpricks of light in the primeval darkness. They chewed roots and fungi that slewed their thoughts and sent their minds into intoxicated delusions. Their tales were of charging rhinos, ferocious sabre-toothed tigers, close shaves with dangerous beasts. Our tales are of rotten ice, desperate struggles in a vertical world, fingers slipping from tiny ledges. On the surface they are different but underneath they are all the same – they are tales of life and death. They talk of what it is to be human in a hostile world. I just hope I'm going to live to tell this one.

As Joe blows cigarette smoke into the air, my gaze alights on the massive jumble of ice that is the Bossons Glacier, and then wanders on up to the summit. I can't help thinking how far away it looks.

* * *

A few days later, after playing at ice climbing on one of the mountain's glaciers, we decide that there is nothing for it but to take on the beast itself. We approach the mountain as we have all others, with the view that we have to climb it from the bottom to the top. There will be no cheating by using cable cars to get out of the valley. Joe and I hike directly up from the village.

It will be a three-day climb. On the first day, we will climb up through the forest and establish ourselves beside where the little mountain railway ends. On the second day we will have to make it the Refuge du Gouter, a climbers' shelter perched high on the mountain within striking distance of its summit. On the third we shall climb to the summit of the mountain and return to the valley.

On the first day, after hours of toil up from the valley floor, Joe and I settle in to our tent a thousand feet below the snowline. We're camped in an Alpine meadow of close-cropped grass. The climb out of the deep valley and on to the shoulder of the mountain has exhausted us, and we fall into a dreamless sleep.

I wake suddenly. There's something moving outside the tent – something big, sniffing and grunting.

"What the hell's that?" Joe whispers.

There's another snuffle and something prods the tent. The

hair on the back of my neck stands up and I begin to sweat with terror.

"It's a bear!"

"They don't have bears in the Alps!" I declare between clenched teeth.

"You sure?"

I'm an avid watcher of wildlife documentaries. My mind races through all the ones I've seen on bears and mountain habitats. Images of bears tearing big holes in flimsy tents flash through my mind. Black bears and grizzly bears live in North America – at least that's where Yogi Bear came from, but that's about all I'm sure of right now. Where is David Attenborough when you need him? I'm beginning to doubt my credentials as a naturalist when something furry brushes against the tent and I realise that there's at least two or three creatures out there.

"There's a few of them. It's okay, bears don't hunt in packs," I inform Joe as if I'm passing on the best news he'll ever hear.

"Are you sure?" he whispers, hunting in the darkness for his torch.

"Yes, I'm sure." I'm just beginning to relax as my confidence grows until another thought punctures my world. "Wolves! Wolves hunt in packs."

"Shit." Joe's face is suddenly illuminated in torchlight. Cautiously he begins to pull down the door zip to look outside. He only gets the zip a few inches down when a black nose juts through the opening. We both howl in terror. A pinks tongue follows the nose and gives Joe's face an enormous, affectionate lick.

I collapse back on my sleeping bag howling with laughter.

"It's the dogs from the farmhouse we passed a while ago."

"I nearly pissed myself." Joe takes a little longer to see the funny side.

The following morning we begin the climb in earnest. Once above the snowline the intensity of the Alpine sunlight takes us by surprise. The air is so clear that the sun has little to filter its rays, and light bounces back off the snow with amazing power. We are heading up to where the Gouter hut sits perched, incredibly, on the massive shoulder of the mountain. We will spend the night there and set off before dawn the following morning, if we can get there that is. We are crossing a huge snowfield leading to a rocky ridge that seems to climb into the sky. On a massive glacier below us, huge blocks of ice glisten in the sun, each capable of crushing a house with ease.

At last we reach the base of the rock ridge that leads up to the hut. The hut is a strange, alien structure, all gleaming aluminium, as though some Martian space traveller has carelessly abandoned it high on the mountain. The ridge is broken rock and snow, relatively easy climbing but very exposed. Here and there are brass crosses that have been driven into the rock, recording the names of climbers who have fallen to their deaths. Joe and I rope up and climb the ridge slowly and carefully. The crosses come in handy for belays.

Oddly, amongst all this ice and snow, it's the heat that gets to us. The sun is unrelenting and we sip on our meagre rations of water. Joe has a rather snazzy pair of mirrored sunglasses to protect his eyes from the glare. I couldn't afford such luxury and am wearing what appear to be welder's goggles, giving me the appearance of a startled frog. I've smeared white glacier cream

– a sort of barrier cream made from lard – all over my face and am gently frying. We have been climbing the ridge for over two hours but the gleaming hut appears no closer than when we began.

"Christ, how far is it?" Joe asks…

~

20014355R00130

Printed in Great Britain
by Amazon